# 400 Sea Food

## Recipes

## 947993 -- BAKED CLAMS

2 doz. clams  
4 tbsp. olive oil  
2 cloves garlic, minced  
1 med. onion, chopped  
1 tbsp. bread crumbs  
1 tsp. parsley or chives  
1/4 tsp. oregano  
Salt & pepper  
Grated Parmesan cheese  
Lemon juice  

Scrub clams with stiff brush under cold water until all grit is removed. Saute onion and garlic until golden. Remove clams from shell (steam open). Chop up clams very fine, mix with bread crumbs, parsley, salt, pepper and oregano. Fill shells. Sprinkle with cheese and lemon juice. Dot with butter and place under hot broiler about 5 minutes.

------------------------

## 947994 -- SEAFOOD FANCIES

8 oz. can Pillsbury refrigerator  
   butterflake dinner rolls  
7 1/2 oz. can crab meat, rinsed &  
   drained  
2 1/2 oz. can tiny shrimp, rinsed &  
   drained  
1 c. shredded Swiss cheese  
1/2 c. mayonnaise  
1 tbsp. chopped onion  
1 tbsp. chopped pimento  
1/2 tsp. parsley flakes  
1/4 tsp. curry powder  
8 oz. can water chestnuts, drained &  
   sliced  

Heat oven to 400 degrees. Lightly grease cookie sheets. Separate dough into 12 pieces. Separate each piece into 3 equal layers. Place on prepared cookie sheets. In small bowl, combine crab, shrimp, cheese, mayonnaise, onion, pimento, parsley flakes and curry powder. Spoon teaspoonful seafood mixture onto each dough piece; top with several slices of water chestnuts. Bake at 400 degrees for 10 to 12 minutes or until light golden brown. Serve hot, refrigerate leftovers. Makes 36.

------------------------

947995 -- NOEL KIRK ERICKSON'S SARDINE ROLLS

2 cans of sardines in mustard sauce
1 (8 oz.) pkg. cream cheese
2 hard boiled eggs
2 loaves of sliced white bread
Lemon juice
Mayonnaise
Worcestershire sauce

Mash sardines. Mix together sardines, cream cheese and hard boiled eggs. Add desired amount of lemon juice, mayonnaise, Worcestershire sauce and mix well.
Cut off bread crusts. Spread mixture on slices of bread, roll up and hold together with toothpicks. Broil until toasted.

------------------------

947996 -- SEVICHE SEAFOOD SHELLS

1/2 lb. bay scallops
1/4 c. fresh lime juice
1/3 c. diced med. bell pepper
1/3 c. thinly sliced green onions
1 tbsp. fresh minced cilantro or 1
    tsp. dried
1 tsp. olive oil
1/8 tsp. salt
1/8 tsp. pepper
3 drops hot sauce
16 cooked jumbo macaroni shells

Cook scallops in small amount of boiling water for 1 minute. Drain. Combine scallops and fresh lime juice in small bowl. Toss well. Cover and refrigerate for 1 hour. Add next 7 ingredients. Stir well. Cover and chill 30 minutes.
Drain. Stuff each macaroni shell with 1 tablespoon scallop mixture. Arrange on serving platter.

------------------------

947997 -- SHRIMP BUTTER

2 cans shrimp, broken
1 tbsp. onion, minced
Juice of 1 lemon
4 tbsp. mayonnaise

1 1/2 sticks soft butter
Salt to taste
1 (8 oz.) pkg. cream cheese

Mix all ingredients well with mixer, adding shrimp last. Makes a large amount, and freezes well. This is a spread rather than a dip. I serve with Club crackers.

------------------------

947998 -- HERRING TIDBITS

2 c. (1 pt.) sour cream
1 (12 oz.) jar herring tidbits in
    wine, undrained, chopped
2 apples, peeled, quartered, cored
    and chopped
1 med. Bermuda onion, quartered and
    chopped
1/2 c. seedless grapes, halved
2 hard-cooked eggs, chopped
Rye rounds

Combine first 4 ingredients in large bowl and mix thoroughly. Cover and refrigerate at least 1 hour. Add grapes and eggs and toss lightly. Turn into dish. Serve with rye rounds. Makes about 4 cups.

------------------------

947999 -- BAR-B-QUED SHRIMP

1 lb. shrimp
Olive oil
Cracked black pepper
Salt
Lemon juice
Tabasco
Lea & Perrin's
Butter

Place whole shrimp, keep shells on, in single layer in oven-proof dish.
Drizzle olive oil on top of shrimp. Pepper shrimp until they are black; when you think you have enough pepper, add more. Add lots of salt, lemon juice, Tabasco and Lea & Perrin's. Remember you are seasoning through the shells. Cut up butter on top of shrimp and broil until shrimp are cooked, 15 to 20 minutes. Be sure and taste to see if they are done. Serve these with newspaper on the table and lots of napkins. Have French bread to sop up the oil and encourage guests to eat the shells, as well, if river

shrimp are used. With cold beer and green salad, you have the makings of a great informal party. Base the amount of shrimp on the number of guests.

------------------------

## 948000 -- SMOKED SALMON ECLAIRS

1/2 c. water
4 tbsp. butter, cut into sm. chunks
1/2 c. flour
2 extra lg. eggs, beaten lightly
1/2 tsp. garlic powder
1/2 tsp. dry dill

--FILLING:--

1/2 lb. cream cheese, softened
   (regular or lite)
1/4 c. sour cream (regular or lowfat)
6 oz. smoked salmon, chopped fine
Juice of 1/2 lemon and grated zest
1 tbsp. fresh dill, minced
Dash of nutmeg
1 tsp. minced garlic
Salt and pepper

Preheat oven to 400 degrees. Combine water and butter in small saucepan, bring to boil over high heat. Add flour all at once; beat vigorously until dough forms ball, pulls away from sides of pan and leaves a thin film on bottom of pan. Transfer to mixing bowl. Save 1 tablespoon of beaten egg. Beat the rest of the egg into the dough in two steps, beating until dough is shiny and smooth.
Put dough in pastry bag with #3 star tip. On lightly greased baking sheet, lay down 3 x 1/2 inch strips about 2 inches apart. Bake 15 minutes until puffed up and brown. Remove from oven. Split in half lengthwise. Reassemble and return to baking sheet. Brush top of each with thin film of reserved egg. Sprinkle on combined garlic powder and dill. Reduce oven to 200 degrees. Return eclairs to oven for 20 minutes until dry and crisp. Remove and cool. Mix filling ingredients together. Season to taste with salt and pepper. Just before serving, spoon filling onto bottom half of eclair and top with top half. Makes about 16. Serves 8.

------------------------

## 948001 -- SALMON MOUSSE WITH CUCUMBER VINAIGRETTE

1/2 c. dry Vermouth
1 env. unflavored gelatin

1 c. smoked salmon, flaked
3 hard-cooked eggs, mashed
3/4 c. sour cream
1/2 c. sliced green onions
1/4 c. fresh parsley, chopped fine
3 tbsp. mayonnaise
1 tsp. prepared horseradish
1 tbsp. lemon juice
1 tsp. finely chopped onion

Combine gelatin and dry Vermouth. Heat gently until dissolved, and set aside to cool. Combine all other ingredients into gelatin mix, blending well. Pour into a 2-cup flat-bottom mold. Chill at least 3 hours or overnight.

--CUCUMBER VINAIGRETTE:--

1 med. unpared cucumber, very thinly
   sliced (about 2 c.)
1 med. green pepper, cut into thin
   strips (about 1 c.)
1/4 c. vinegar
1/4 c. lemon juice
1/4 c. salad oil
1/2 tsp. salt
1/4 tsp. Worcestershire sauce
1/8 tsp. pepper

In medium bowl, combine cucumber slices with green pepper strips. In measuring cup, combine rest of ingredients, mixing well. Pour over cucumber mixture, tossing to coat well. Refrigerate, covered, until well chilled--about 1 hour-tossing occasionally. To serve: Drain dressing from vegetables. Arrange vegetables attractively on large platter. To unmold mousse: Run a spatula around edge of mold; invert onto vegetables. Serve at once, with crackers as appetizer or as salad on bed of lettuce.

------------------------

948002 -- SHRIMP   MOUSSE

1 can cream of shrimp soup
1 (8 oz.) cream cheese
1 pkg. Knox gelatin
1 (10 oz.) box cooked shrimp, thawed
1 c. mayonnaise
1/4 c. finely chopped onion
1/2 c. finely chopped celery

Use double boiler and mix soup, gelatin and cream cheese until melted. Remove from heat and add remaining ingredients. Put in mold and chill at least 8 hours.

------------------------

### 948003 -- LEMON PEPPER SHRIMP AND ZUCCHINI

2 med. sized zucchini
2 tbsp. olive or salad oil
1 lb. shelled or deveined lg. shrimp
1 1/4 tsp. lemon pepper seasoning salt
1/2 tsp. salt

Over medium-high heat in hot oil, cook zucchini, stirring frequently, until zucchini begins to brown and is tender-crisp. With slotted spoon - remove zucchini to bowl. In same skillet, over high heat, cook shrimp, lemon-pepper seasoning salt, and salt, stirring until shrimp are opaque throughout - about 5 minutes. Return zucchini to skillet, heat through.

------------------------

### 948004 -- CRAB CROSTINI

8 oz. crabmeat
1/2 c. diced red bell pepper
2 tbsp. + 2 tsp. mayonnaise
2 tbsp. chopped fresh parsley
1 tbsp. chopped fresh chives
1 tbsp. fresh lime juice
1 tbsp. Dijon mustard
2 tsp. grated Parmesan cheese
4-5 drops hot pepper sauce
4 oz. Italian bread, cut into 16
   slices

Preheat broiler. Line a broiler pan with foil. Blend all ingredients except bread. Spread 1 tbsp. of the mixture on each bread slice. Place the crostini on the broiler pan and broil 4 inches from the heat for 5-6 minutes until lightly browned.

------------------------

### 948005 -- SHRIMP DELIGHT

1 can tomato soup
1 (8 oz.) pkg. cream cheese, softened
1 c. Real mayonnaise

1 pkg. Knox unflavored gelatin
1/4 c. water
1 c. celery, very finely chopped
1/8 c. green onion, very finely
   chopped
2 cans tiny, whole shrimp (drained &
   deveined)

Heat soup and cheese, stirring constantly, until both are mixed well.   Cool.  Stir in mayonnaise.  Dissolve gelatin in water, then add to soup mixture.  Stir in remaining ingredients.  Pour in mold or clear serving dish.  Chill until set.  Serve cold with Wheat Thin crackers.   This is a favorite of our family!

------------------------

948006 -- PICKLED   SALMON

1-2 lbs. salmon, tail filet
1 tbsp. sugar
Dillweed
2 tbsp. coarse salt
1 tsp. black pepper

Clean and pat dry the filet of salmon.  Mix the dry ingredients together.  Place the salmon in a glass dish, skin side up.  Rub the skin thoroughly with half the salt mixture; turn the piece over and rub the flesh with the rest of the salt.   Sprinkle lavishly with dill.  Turn flesh down again; cover fish with  foil or plastic wrap and weight lightly with another dish or a board.  Refrigerate for at least 12 hours or up to three days.  To serve, slice thinly on the diagonal and arrange on rye or dark brown bread.  The same recipe can be used with trout or mackerel (boned).

------------------------

948007 -- SCOTCH   STYLE   PICKLED   SALMON

Cooked salmon, boned and skinned
   (leftover salmon may be used - HA!)
1 c. white wine vinegar
1 tbsp. black peppercorns
8 allspice berries
1/2 c. white wine, or fish stock
1 tsp. white peppercorns
1/2 tsp. coriander seeds

Bring the liquids and spices to a boil in a stainless steel or enameled pan (not aluminum cookware); add 2 teaspoons salt.  Place fish pieces in a wide mouthed jar or a glass dish and cover with hot spiced liquid. Cover the dish and refrigerate for several hours or days. Serve fish, drained, on lettuce with a bland mayonnaise or sour cream with dill.

------------------------

## 948009 -- SEAFOOD CHOWDER

Cook slowly in kettle until fat begins to fry out: 4 tbsp. finely cut pork or bacon

Add and cook over low heat until yellow: 4 tbsp. minced onion

Add: Liquor from 2 (7 oz.) cans minced or
   whole clams, lobster or other seafood
2 c. finely diced potatoes
1/2 c. boiling water

Cook until potatoes are tender, 10 minutes (If potatoes are cooked, omit water). Just before serving, add: Clams or other seafood from 2 (7 oz.)
   cans
2 c. milk
1 tsp. salt
1/8 tsp. pepper

Heat to boiling, stirring occasionally. Serve immediately. Makes 6 servings. Note: butter may be used in place of pork or bacon.

------------------------

## 948010 -- SEASONED OYSTERS

2 lb. box oyster crackers or 2 sm. bags
1 c. oil
2-3 tbsp. dill weed
Garlic powder to taste
1 env. dry Ranch dressing

Combine above ingredients in bowl and enjoy!

------------------------

## 948011 -- SCALLOPED OYSTERS & SCALLOPS

1 qt. oysters
1 pt. scallops
1 c. sour cream

2 c. bread crumbs
1/2 c. melted butter (not oleo)

Mix melted butter and bread crumbs together and put a thin layer in the bottom of a buttered baking dish. Cover with oysters and seasonings, add some cream. Add layer of scallops, seasonings and layer of crumbs. Repeat. Top with buttered crumbs and bake in hot oven (400 degrees) for 30 minutes.

------------------------

## 948012 -- DILL SHRIMP WITH RICE

2 tbsp. mustard (any kind)
20 sm. shrimp, peeled & deveined
3 sliced mushrooms
1 tbsp. chopped fresh dill
1/2 c. wine (chablis or sherry)
1/4 c. cream
Cooked rice
Pinch of garlic

Saute shrimp with mushrooms and dill and garlic until shrimp is done on one side. Turn the shrimp over, and add wine and mustard. Cook 2 minutes. Add cream, cook 1 minute. Put over hot cooked rice. Serves 2 to 4.

------------------------

## 948013 -- SHRIMP, VEGETABLE MELODY

1 to 3 lbs. shrimp, cleaned
Broccoli
Summer squash
Zucchini
Mushrooms
Cherry tomatoes
2 tbsp. butter
Throwaway lasagna pan

Cut vegetables into bite-size pieces. Put shrimp, vegetables, butter, a dash of salt and pepper into pans. Cover with tinfoil double. Put on low grill with cover down. Cook about 35 minutes. Serves 6 to 8.

------------------------

## 948014 -- SHRIMP CREOLE

1 lb. cooked shrimp
2 tbsp. butter
Salt and pepper
Boiled rice
2 c. canned tomatoes
1 minced green pepper
2 minced onions
1/2 c. sliced mushrooms
1/2 c. stock, chicken bouillon cubes
2 tbsp. minced ham
2 tbsp. flour
2 tbsp. butter

Melt the butter and add the shrimp and cook together for 2 minutes. Add to the creole sauce. Simmer for 5 minutes, and serve with boiled rice. For the sauce: Cook the tomatoes, pepper, onion and mushrooms for 10 minutes. Add the stock and ham and cook 2 minutes longer. Thicken with the flour lightly creamed with the butter and stir until thick and smooth. Serves 6.

------------------------

948015 -- SHRIMP   CREOLE

Cooked rice
1/2 c. diced celery
1/4 c. minced onion
1/4 c. diced green pepper
3 tbsp. butter or margarine
1 tbsp. flour
1 tsp. salt
1 tsp. sugar
Dash of pepper
16 oz. can tomatoes
1 bay leaf
1 sprig parsley
3/4 lb. shrimp

Saute celery, onion and green pepper in butter in sauce pan until tender but not brown. Blend in flour, salt, sugar and pepper. Stir in tomatoes, add bay leaf and parsley. Simmer for 30 minutes. Remove bay leaf. Add shrimp, heat thoroughly and serve over hot rice.

------------------------

948016 -- SALMON   AUGRATIN

1 can red salmon
2 c. white sauce
1/2 lb. sharp cheese
1 c. Wheaties
Oleo or butter

Butter baking dish put small amount of white sauce on the bottom. Add salmon and remaining white sauce. Top with grated sharp cheese and Wheaties. *Dot with oleo or butter and bake 20 minutes at 325 to 350 degrees. Serves 4 to 6.

------------------------

948017 -- CRAB   IMPERIAL

1/4 green pepper, diced
2 tbsp. diced pimiento
1 tbsp. dry mustard
1/2 tsp. salt
1/8 tsp. black pepper
2 eggs
1 lb. backfin crabmeat
1/2 c. mayonnaise
Dash of red pepper

Blend crabmeat and other ingredients. Heap lightly in four baking shells or crabshells. Top with mayonnaise and sprinkle with paprika. Bake at 350 degrees for 15 minutes.

------------------------

948018 -- EASY   IMPERIAL   CRAB

2 lb. crab meat, backfin
1/3 green pepper, cut fine
3/4 red pimiento, chopped
1 tsp. mustard
1/3 c. mayonnaise
1 egg
1/8 tsp. pepper
1 tsp. salt
Mayonnaise for topping

Mix all ingredients except crab meat. Add crab meat carefully in order not to break up lumps. Pile into 6 baking shells (heaping) spread with mayonnaise and sprinkle with paprika. Bake at 350 degrees for 20 minutes.

------------------------

### 948019 -- CRAB IMPERIAL C.'S

1 lb. lump crab meat, picked over for
  shell
1/2 c. minced green bell pepper
1/4 c. minced onion
3/4 c. mayonnaise
3 tbsp. butter, melted
1/2 c. fresh bread crumbs

Combine the crabmeat, peppers and onion and gently fold in the mayonnaise. Mold the mixture into a clean crab shell or heat proof serving dish and cover with melted butter and bread crumbs. Bake at 350 degrees for 12 minutes or until crumbs are golden brown. Serve at once. Serves 4.

------------------------

### 948020 -- CRAB FETTUCINI

6 oz. fettucini
4 tbsp. margarine
2 cloves garlic, minced
1 c. milk
1/2 lb. crab, flaked
1/4 c. parmesan cheese
Pepper to taste

Cook fettucini according to package. In skillet, saute garlic in margarine. Add milk, crab and pepper. Heat until bubbling, about 3 minutes. Add parmesan cheese and stir 1 minute. Toss with cooked fettucini. Serves 4.

------------------------

### 948021 -- ORANGE ROUGHY

2 lbs. orange roughy fillets
1/2 c. sliced almonds
1/4 c. parsley, minced
1/4 c. margarine, melted
2 tsp. lemon or lime juice
1 tsp. salt
1/4 tsp. pepper

Combine margarine and almonds. Saute almonds to a golden brown. Arrange fish, single layered, in a shallow baking pan.  Sprinkle with lemon or lime juice.  Spoon almond-margarine mixture over fish.  Sprinkle with salt, pepper and parsley.  Bake, covered, at 350 degrees for 10 minutes.  Bake, uncovered, until fish flakes easily with fork, about 8 to 10 minutes.   Serve with lemon or lime   wedges.

------------------------

948022 -- CAJUN   SHRIMP

 1/2 c. olive oil
2 tbsp. cajun seasoning
2 tbsp. lemon juice
2 tbsp. fresh parsley, chopped
1 tbsp. honey
1 tbsp. soy sauce
Pinch cayenne pepper
1 lb. shrimp, uncooked, shelled and
   deveined

Combine first seven ingredients in a 9" x 13" baking dish.  Add shrimp and toss to coat.  Refrigerate at least 1 hour.  Preheat oven to 450 degrees.  Bake until shrimp are cooking through, stirring occasionally, about 10 minutes.  I sometimes serve with fettucini alfredo and French bread.

------------------------

948023 -- EASY   SHRIMP   NEWBURG

 1 (10 3/4 oz.) can cream of shrimp soup
3/4 c. evaporated milk
1 1/2 c. shrimp, cooked
1 (4 oz.) can mushrooms, drained and
   sliced
2 tbsp. dry sherry
2 egg yolks, beaten

Place all ingredients, except egg yolks, in crock pot.  Stir thoroughly.  Cover and cook on low for 4 to 6 hours.  Add yolks during last hour.  Serve over hot rice or in puff pastry shells.  Serves 4.  Lobster Newburg:  5 ounces frozen lobster, flaked, may be substituted for shrimp.

------------------------

948024 -- SHRIMP   SCAMPI

 1/2 c. oleo

2 tbsp. parsley
2 tbsp. lemon juice
2 cloves garlic, minced
1 1/2 lbs. shrimp, cleaned and shelled

Saute garlic in melted oleo for 1 to 2 minutes in microwave. Add parsley and lemon juice. Add shrimp; toss to coat. Microwave on high for 3 to 5 1/2 minutes, stirring after 4 minutes. Serve with rice or pasta tossed with parsley and parmesan cheese.

------------------------

948025 -- SOLE WITH SHRIMP

1 1/2 lbs. sole fillets
2 c. light cream
1/2 c. sherry
Salt and pepper
1/2 c. fresh or canned shrimp,
   drained and cooked
1/2 c. buttered bread crumbs

Trim fillets and place in a shallow, greased, glass baking dish. Add the cream and sherry. Season with salt and pepper. Add shrimp. Bake in a hot 400 degree oven until cream and sherry have thickened and cooked down. Sprinkle with buttered bread crumbs over the surface. Place under broiler until sauce bubbles and browns in spots. Can add lemon slices or parsley for a garnish.

------------------------

948026 -- SPICY SHRIMP

2 - 3 lbs. lg. shrimp in shell, split
   and deveined
2 lemons, thinly sliced
1 lb. butter
3/4 tsp. dried rosemary
3/4 tsp. dried basil
1/2 c. worcestershire sauce
2 tsp. salt
3 tbsp. freshly ground black pepper
3/4 tsp. tabasco sauce
3 cloves garlic, peeled and lightly
   crushed

In large, shallow glass baking dish, place shrimp in single layer. Cover with sliced lemon. In saucepan, heat remaining ingredients to boiling. Pour over shrimp and lemons, cover and marinate overnight in refrigerator. Bring shrimp to room temperature before cooking. Bake shrimp in preheated 450 degree oven for 20 minutes. Serve as appetizer or entree with crusty French bread.

------------------------

## 948027 -- SALMON OR TUNA BAKED POTATOES

1 can salmon, or 2 cans tuna, drained
4 baking potatoes, cleaned
1/2 c. milk
1/4 c. margarine
1/2 c. parmesan cheese, grated
1/4 c. green onion, minced
1 tsp. thyme
1 tsp. dill
1 tsp. salt
1 tsp. pepper
1/4 c. frozen peas, thawed

Bake potatoes. When cool, cut in half and scoop out centers. Mash potatoes and beat in cheese, onion and spices. Stir in salmon or tuna and peas. Spoon mixture back into hollowed out skins. Bake at 350 degrees for 20 minutes.

------------------------

## 948028 -- FRESH SCALLOPS

1 lb. fresh scallops
1/2 c. oil
1/2 tsp. thyme
1/2 c. dry white wine
3 cloves garlic
1/2 c. butter
2 tbsp. fresh parsley, chopped

Dredge scallops in flour. Heat oil in large skillet with butter; add crushed garlic and brown. As soon as garlic browns, add scallops and saute until lightly colored. Add white wine at last minute and simmer. Serve immediately.

------------------------

## 948029 -- SCALLOPS PROVENCIAL

1 1/2 lbs. scallops
1/2 c. flour

2 tbsp. oil
4 tbsp. margarine
1 clove garlic, peeled and finely
   minced
2 tbsp. fresh lemon juice
1/2 c. parsley, finely minced
Salt and pepper, to taste
4 slices crisp toast

Wash and dry the scallops. Roll in flour. Heat oil with margarine and garlic over medium heat. Add scallops. Stir-fry until firm, white and flecked with brown. Add lemon juice and parsley. Season with salt and pepper. Stir to blend and serve at once over crisp toast or serve with cooked rice. Serves 4.

------------------------

### 948030 -- FILLETS OF SOLE MARGUERY

8 fillets of sole or flounder
1 lobster, boiled
18 little-neck clams, or fresh mussels
1 lb. shrimp
1/2 c. dry sherry
3 tbsp. butter
3 tbsp. flour
Salt
Pepper
Parmesan cheese

Boil lobster, save water to use for poaching clams or mussels and shrimp.
After all are prepared, reserve 1 cup of stock. Sprinkle fillets with salt and paprika and 1/2 cup dry sherry, cover, and bake for 15 minutes at 350 degrees.
Melt butter, stir in flour, add strained stock, and boil until thickened. Stir in 1/4 cup liquid from baking dish. Salt and pepper to taste. Pour sauce over fillets. Garnish with clams, lobster meat and shrimp. Sprinkle with parmesan cheese. Bake until heated through. Broil until golden. Serve.

------------------------

### 948031 -- SEAFOOD QUICHE

1 unbaked pastry shell, regular size
   baking shell
1/2 lb. sliced Swiss cheese
1/2 c. sm. shrimp

4 oz. frozen canned crabmeat

Line pastry shell with double slices of cheese. Cover cheese with a layer of shrimp and a layer of crabmeat. Beat together: 2 beaten eggs
1 c. whipping cream
1/2 tbsp. flour
1/4 tsp. salt
1/4 tsp. pepper
1/4 tsp. cayenne

Combine the above with: 1 tbsp. sherry wine
1 tbsp. melted butter

Pour mixture over seafood. This may now be refrigerated or frozen. To serve: Bake for 40 minutes at 375 degrees until light brown. Quiche should stand for at least 20 minutes before serving. Administrator (1980-1992)

------------------------

## 948032 -- LINGUINI WITH SEAFOOD, SUN DRIED TOMATOES & LEMON

1 lb. linguini
1/4 c. olive oil
1 stick butter
4 garlic cloves, minced
1 lb. shrimp, peeled
1 lb. sea scallops
1 bottle clam juice
1/3 c. sun dried tomato paste
1/4 c. minced fresh parsley
Peel from 1 lemon removed in strips
Salt & red pepper flakes

Melt butter and olive oil in heavy pot, add garlic and saute until tender. Add shrimp and scallops and saute until shrimp turns pink and scallops are almost cooked about 10 minutes. Add clam juice, salt and pepper. Add cooked linguini cook about 3 minutes more. Add tomatoes, parsley, lemon peel to pasta and toss. Serve immediately (you may add canned minced clams, black olives, artichokes in oil, whatever else you like). Grandmother

------------------------

## 948033 -- FETTUCINI WITH SMOKED SALMON

1 lb. fettucini (green if available)

1 oz. (2 tbsp.) butter
Half of a sm. onion
5 oz. smoked salmon
7 fl. oz. heavy cream
Black pepper

Melt the butter and cook the finely chopped onion until it is soft but has not changed color. Add half the smoked salmon, roughly chopped and the cream. Warm gently, then blend or process together with the onion until smooth. Cut the rest of the salmon into thin strips, using kitchen scissors. Cook the pasta, according to package directions carefully to avoid over cooking. Drain the pasta and turn into a serving bowl. Add the cream and salmon sauce. Stir thoroughly and add a little freshly ground black pepper. Gently stir in the salmon strips and serve at once.    Cheshire, CT

------------------------

948034 -- SHRIMP   MARINARA

1/2 c. olive oil
3 lg. onions
1 clove galric
1 1/2 lb. uncooked, unshelled shrimps
1 pt. Marsala or other light, sweet
   red wine
1/4 tsp. salt
1/8 tsp. pepper
1 sm. can Italian plum tomatoes
1/2 can tomato paste
1 can chicken broth
1 tbsp. chopped parsley
4 tbsp. (1/2 stick) butter

Cut onions in small pieces. Mince galric. Saute in olive oil until yellow. Add shrimps in shells. Let simmer 5 minutes. Add wine, according to taste. Season with salt and pepper; simmer 10 more minutes over moderate heat. Remove shrimps from sauce with slotted spoon. Shell and save. Stir in tomatoes and tomato paste and cook 5 minutes over moderate heat. Mash everything together with potato masher. Add broth and simmer slowly for an hour, until sauce is very thick. When ready to serve return shelled shrimps to sauce, add parsley and butter. As soon as butter melts it is ready to serve. Good on rice or pasta. Serves 4.

------------------------

948035 -- CRAB   SOUFFLE

1 1/4 c. melted butter

12 slices white bread
2 (7 oz.) cans white crab meat
   ("Madam" brand)
1 lb. sliced Cheddar cheese
6 eggs
2 1/2 c. milk
Salt & pepper to taste

Cut crust off of bread and dip both sides in melted butter. Place 6 slices across bottom of rectangular serving pan (13 x 9 x 2 inches or larger). Cover with 1/2 of crab and 1/2 of cheese. Cover with remaining slices of bread dipped in butter, then crab and cheese. Let set in refrigerator for 24 hours. Bake at 350 degrees for 1 hour. Serves 6-8.

------------------------

948036 -- HONOLULU  SHRIMP  WITH  RICE

4 strips bacon, diced
1/2 lb. ground beef
1 c. finely chopped onion
3 c. cooked rice
2 c. cleaned cooked shrimp
1/3 c. minced celery leaves
1/2 tsp. salt
1/4 tsp. dry mustard
Dash pepper
3 tbsp. soy sauce
3 bananas, slightly green

Cook bacon crisp. Add ground beef and onions. Cook until onions are tender. Add remaining ingredients, except bananas. Mix heat thoroughly. Slice bananas, brown lightly in butter. Serve rice-shrimp in a bowl. Border with bananas.

------------------------

948037 -- LOUISIANA  SHRIMP  CREOLE

1 or more sticks butter or margarine
8 tbsp. flour
1 c. chopped parsley
1 doz. green onions, chopped
1 green pepper, chopped
8-9 cloves garlic, chopped
4 lb. or more shrimp
1/2 stalk celery, chopped

2 med. onions, chopped
6 c. water
3 cans tomato paste
1 tsp. sugar
2 tbsp. salt
1 tsp. pepper, black

1/2 tsp. red pepper
2 tbsp. Worcestershire sauce
1 tsp. Tabasco sauce
1 tsp. vinegar

Cook butter and flour until browned; add vegetables. Saute 10-15 minutes. Add water and remaining ingredients except vinegar and shrimp. Simmer 30 minutes. Add vinegar and simmer 1 hour and 30 minutes. Add shrimp and bring to a boil and simmer 20 minutes. Serve over hot rice. (I add more shrimp than is called for.)

------------------------

## 948038 -- SEAFOOD QUICHE

1 unbaked pie shell
1 lb. fresh or frozen shrimp, peeled
   & deveined
3 eggs
1 c. half & half
1 c. grated Swiss cheese
1/2 tsp. salt
1 tsp. pepper
3/4 c. onion, chopped
2 tbsp. butter

Cook shrimp and drain. Mix eggs, cream, cheese, salt and pepper. Saute onions in butter until soft. Add to egg mixture along with shrimp. Pour into pie shell. Bake at 350 degrees for 40-45 minutes. Serves 6. I use half fresh or frozen shrimp and the rest canned crab.

------------------------

## 948039 -- VIVIAN'S SEAFOOD NEWBURG

1 (10 oz.) pkg. frozen green beans
    (can use can beans but they
  are not as pretty)
3/4 lb. fresh or frozen shrimp
3/4 lb. fresh or frozen scallops

1 c. water
1 c. sliced fresh mushrooms
2 tbsp. thin sliced green onion
1 tbsp. margarine or butter
1/4 tsp. salt
2 tbsp. all-purpose flour
1/8 tsp. ground nutmeg
1/8 tsp. pepper
1 c. water
1/2 c. nonfat dry powdered milk
1 beaten egg white
2 tbsp. dry white wine
3/4 c. soft bread crumbs
2 tbsp. grated Parmesan
1 tbsp. margarine or butter

Cook and drain green beans according to directions on package. Combine thawed shrimp, scallops and 1 cup water. Bring to boil; reduce heat, cover and simmer 2-3 minutes until scallops and shrimp are opaque. Drain. In a skillet cook mushrooms and green onion in 1 tablespoon margarine about 5 minutes or until tender. Stir in flour, salt, nutmeg and pepper. Add water and nonfat dry powdered milk. Cook and stir until thickened and bubbly. Remove from heat. Gradually stir in 1 cup hot mixture into beaten egg white until blended. Return to remaining hot mixture in skillet. Add wine and fish, stir until bubbly. Spoon over green beans. Toss bread crumbs and Parmesan cheese together. Add melted margarine. Sprinkle over other mixture. Bake in 400 degree oven about 10 minutes until brown.

------------------------

948040 -- MYRA'S SHRIMP SPAGHETTI

6 oz. spaghetti
2 (14 1/2 oz.) cans stewed tomatoes
1 (6 oz.) can tomato paste
1/2 c. chopped onion
1 tsp. dried oregano, crushed
1 tsp. dried basil, crushed
1/4-1/2 crushed red pepper
1/4 tsp. garlic powder
1/4 tsp. dried thyme
1 (16 oz.) pkg. frozen peeled
   deveined shrimp (or fresh)
1/2 c. chopped green pepper

Cook spaghetti according to directions on package; drain and keep warm. In saucepan combine undrained tomatoes, tomato paste, onion, oregano, basil, red pepper, garlic powder and thyme. Cook uncovered over medium-low heat 10 minutes until mixture is somewhat thickened, stirring occasionally. Add shrimp and green pepper, cook uncovered 10 minutes until shrimp are no longer pink, stirring occasionally. Serve over spaghetti. Serves 6. This is a low cal/low fat meal.

------------------------

948041 -- SHRIMP   SUPREME

2 lb. shrimp, cooked & peeled
2 c. rice, cooked
1 c. mayonnaise
2 c. cream of chicken soup
1 pkg. green onion soup mix
2 c. Cheddar cheese, grated

Combine all ingredients except cheese and mix well. Pour into lightly greased casserole and top with cheese. Bake at 350 degrees for about 10 minutes or until bubbly. Serves 6.

------------------------

948042 -- SEAFOOD   AUGRATIN

4 (1 lb.) lobsters or (1 1/2 lbs.
   shrimp) or crab
1/4 lb. butter
1 c. sliced mushrooms
1/2 c. white wine or sherry
2 tbsp. flour
1 tsp. salt
1/8 tsp. white pepper
1 c. heavy cream
1/2 c. gruyere cheese, grated

Melt 6 tablespoons butter. Saute seafood 3 minutes. Add mushrooms, saute 2 minutes. Add wine. Cook over low heat 5 minutes. Mix flour, salt, and pepper with cream. Add to seafood stirring until boiling point. Place in casserole dish, sprinkle with cheese, dot with remaining butter. Cook at 400 degrees for 10 minutes. Serve over rice. Serves 4.

------------------------

948043 -- NOVA'S   SHRIMP

2 c. cooked rice

1 lb. shrimp
4 slices bacon
2 green onion tops, chopped
Salt and pepper to taste
Soy sauce to taste
MSG to taste

Brown bacon, drain well on paper towel. Cook shrimp in bacon drippings until pink. Add rice, crumbled bacon, and chopped onion. Add seasonings. Stir well.

------------------------

948044 -- SEAFOOD LASAGNA

Bake 1 hour and 45 minutes. Yield: 12 servings. Delicious! 9 uncooked dried lasagna noodles

--SAUCE:--

3 tbsp. butter
1/4 c. all-purpose flour
2 tsp. finely chopped garlic
1 1/2 c. milk
1/2 c. dry white wine or milk
1 tsp. nutmeg
1/2 tsp. salt
1/4 tsp. pepper
1/8 tsp. hot pepper sauce

--RICOTTA FILLING:--

2 eggs
3/4 c. Parmesan cheese, grated
1/2 c. chopped fresh parsley
1 (15 oz.) carton (2 c.) Ricotta
    cheese
1 (4 oz.) jar sliced pimiento, drained

--LAYERS:--

1 (12 oz.) pkg. sm. frozen, cooked
    shrimp, thawed and drained
1 (8 oz.) pkg. frozen, salad chunks
    imitation sea stixs, thawed and
    drained
3 c. (12 oz.) shredded Swiss cheese

12 fresh parsley sprigs

Heat oven to 375 degrees. Cook noodles according to package directions; rinse. Drain; set aside. In 2 quart saucepan melt butter over medium heat. Stir in flour and garlic until bubbly (1 minute). Stir in 1 1/2 cups milk. Continue cooking, stirring occasionally, until mixture comes to a full boil (4 to 5 minutes); boil 1 minute. Stir in remaining sauce ingredients; set aside. In small bowl, slightly beat eggs; stir in all remaining Ricotta filling ingredients. In greased 13 x 9 inch baking pan layer 1/3 noodles, 1/2 Ricotta filling, 1/2 shrimp, 1/2 sea stixs, 1/3 sauce sauce and 1/3 Swiss cheese.
Repeat layering. Top with remaining noodles, sauce and Swiss cheese. Cover with aluminum foil; bake 25 minutes. Uncover; continue baking 15 to 20 minutes or until lightly browned. Let stand 10 minutes. 1 serving: Calories 370, protein 28g, carbohydrates 20g, fat 18g, cholesterol 150mg, sodium 483mg. You can use "light" Ricotta cheese, skim milk to reduce fat and calorie intake.

------------------------

948045 -- FLOUNDER WITH CREAM OF SHRIMP SOUP

1 pkg. frozen flounder
Salt and pepper to taste
Worcestershire sauce
1 can cream of shrimp soup
Tabasco sauce
1 oz. sherry

Salt and pepper dish. Place in casserole dish and cover with Worcestershire sauce. Pour soup on top. Heat at 350 degrees until bubbly. Add a dash of Tabasco sauce and sherry. Cook about 30-40 minutes.

------------------------

948046 -- TERIYAKI-GRILLED SWORDFISH OR SALMON

2/3 c. soy sauce (med. salt)
1/2 c. med.-dry sherry
1 tbsp. sugar
1 garlic clove, crushed
2 tsp. ginger
2 lbs. swordfish or salmon

In a saucepan, combine soy sauce, sherry, sugar, garlic, and ginger. Bring to boil over moderate heat. Place in a shallow glass pan. Marinate fish for about 30 minutes, turning several times. Cook on well-oiled grill, 10 minutes per inch of thickness and brush frequently with marinade. Use marinade as a dipping sauce or pour over rice for good flavor.

------------------------

### 948047 -- SALMON PATTIES

2 tbsp. oil
1 lg. can salmon or 2 cans Chicken of the Sea boneless and skinless salmon
1/2 sm. onion, chopped finely
1 tsp. margarine
Salt, pepper or Mrs. Dash
4 tbsp. water ground cornmeal
4 tbsp. flour

In a heavy saucepan, melt margarine and cook onions. Mix together salmon, onion, Mrs. Dash, cornmeal and flour. Make into patties. Use 2 tablespoons of oil and fry patties.

------------------------

### 948048 -- SALMON WELLINGTON

4 oz. boneless, skinless salmon
3 oz. duxelle
3 oz. puff dough

Brown salmon quickly on both sides in hot oil. Let cool. Coat salmon with duxelle. Roll dough to a square, 4 x 5 inch, about 1/8 inch thick. Wrap dough around fish, which is covered with duxelle. Refrigerate over an hour then brush with egg wash. Cooking time is 15 minutes in the oven at 425 degrees, or until golden brown.

CEE AAC Phoenix Country Club

------------------------

### 948049 -- HONEY MUSTARD SCALLOPS

2 lbs. sea scallops
1 lb. very lean bacon
1 box sesame seeds
1 jar honey mustard

Rinse scallops with cold water and then if very large cut in half. Pat dry and roll in sesame seeds. Cut bacon strips in half; roll sesame coated scallop in 1/2 slice of bacon. Place on cookie sheet. Bake at 375 degrees until bacon is crisp. Use honey mustard as a side dip. Serves 6 to 8. Parent

------------------------

948050 -- SHRIMP STRATA

Layer: 1. Mix 8 ounces cream cheese and 8 ounces sour cream  2. 3 (6 1/2 oz.) cans tiny shrimp  3. 1 large bottle of cocktail sauce  4. 8 ounces grated Mozzarella cheese  5. Mix together 1 green pepper, chopped, 1 bunch scallions, chopped and 1 large tomato, chopped. Refrigerate covered in a 10" quiche pan. Serves 8 to 10. Parent

------------------------

948051 -- CRAB APPLE JELLY

7 c. prepared crab apple juice
9 c. sugar
1 box Sure Jell fruit pectin

Use fully ripe crab apples. Wash and remove stems. Place in 6 or 8 quart boiler; cover with water and boil 15 to 20 minutes. Let cool; to extract juice, place crab apples in dampened jelly bag or several thicknesses of cheesecloth. Let drip; when dripping gently press or squeeze bag. Measure sugar and set aside. Measure juice and Sure Jell. Bring to a full boil over high heat, stirring constantly. At once stir in sugar and bring to a full rolling boil that cannot be stirred down; boil hard for 5 minutes, stirring constantly. Remove from heat, skim off foam with large metal spoon. Immediately put into hot jars and seal. Pineland, TX

------------------------

948052 -- PASTA AND SEAFOOD MARINARA

1 (16 oz.) can crushed tomatoes
3 tbsp. olive oil
1/2 sm. diced onion
6-8 oz. fresh mushrooms, diced

Salt and pepper to taste
2 tbsp. parsley
2 tsp. oregano
1/4 c. white wine
1 lb. raw shrimp
1/2 lb. raw lg. scallops

Place oil in large frying pan, cook onions and mushrooms until soft. Add salt and pepper. Simmer 10 minutes. Add can of tomatoes, parsley, oregano, and wine. Simmer 10 more minutes. Add seafood (amounts of shrimp and scallops may be altered, according to your own taste, as long as the total equals 1 1/2 pounds). Cook until shrimp are pink and curled and scallops are soft. Serve over angel hair or linguini.

------------------------

948053 -- GRILLED   ALASKA   SALMON

Salmon steaks or fillets
Oil or basting sauce

Place salmon steaks or fillets on hot, well-oiled grill. Grill, allowing 10 minutes per inch of thickness measured at its thickest part; turn once. Thoroughly brush salmon with oil or basting sauce several times during grilling. Grill until salmon flakes easily with a fork at its thickest part.

------------------------

948054 -- BAKED   SCALLOPS

1 1/2 lb. scallops
1/2 tsp. salt
1/2 tsp. pepper
1/2 tsp. cayenne pepper (optional)
1 c. bread crumbs
1 egg
2 tbsp. milk
1/2 c. margarine, melted
Bread crumbs

Mix dry ingredients together. Beat egg and milk together. Dip scallops in crumb mixture, egg mixture, and again in crumbs. Place dipped scallops in roasting pan and drizzle melted margarine over all. Bake at 450 degrees for 25-30 minutes.

------------------------

948055 -- SEAFOOD   CASSEROLE   (MICROWAVE)

1/2 lb. cod, haddock, pollock fillets, cut into pieces of the same size
3 sm. tomatoes, chopped
2 sm. green peppers, chopped
1 tsp. parsley
1/2 tsp. thyme
2 tsp. paprika
1 bay leaf
1/2 c. white wine
1/2 lb. pollock fillets, cut into pieces of the same size
1/2 c. chopped onion
1/2 c. chopped celery
1/2 tsp. black pepper
1/2 tsp. seafood seasoning
1/4 c. water
3 tbsp. margarine
2 1/2 tbsp. flour

In a 4-quart casserole dish, melt margarine on medium high (80%) power for 45 seconds or until it melts. Add flour, stir, cover and cook on medium high (80%) power for 1 minute. Stir and reset for 30 seconds, stir and reset for 15 seconds. Add onion, pepper, celery, spices, wine and water. Mix together well, cover, cook at high power (100%) for 2 minutes. Add tomatoes, stir. Cook for 2 minutes at high power (100%). Reduce to medium (70%) heat, cover and cook for 10 minutes. Stir every 3 minutes. Place pieces of fish on top, cover and cook at high power (100%) for 4 minutes. Stir, serve with bread. Serves 5.

------------------------

948056 -- SHRIMP STROGANOFF

1 lb. lg. shrimp
3 tbsp. butter or margarine
1/2 lb. mushrooms
2 tbsp. dry sherry
2 tubes. all-purpose flour
1/8 tsp. pepper
1 env. chicken-flavor bouillon
1 (8 oz.) container sour cream
2 tsp. minced parsley for garnish

ABOUT 45 MINUTES BEFORE SERVING: Shell and devein shrimp; rinse with running cold water and pat dry with paper towels. In 10-inch skillet over medium-high heat, in 2 tablespoons hot butter or margarine (1/4 stick), cook shrimp, stirring frequently, until shrimp turn pink and are tender, about 5 minutes. With slotted spoon, remove shrimp to bowl. To drippings in skillet, add 1 more tablespoon hot butter or margarine. Add mushrooms and sherry; cook, stirring frequently, until mushrooms are tender. In cup, stir flour, pepper, bouillon, and 1 cup water until blended; stir into mushrooms. Cook mushroom mixture, stirring constantly, until sauce boils and thickens slightly. Reduce heat to low; stir in sour cream until blended. Return shrimp to skillet and cook over low heat, stirring, until shrimp are hot; do not boil. Pour Stroganoff into serving bowl; garnish with parsley. Rice makes a perfect complement. Makes 4 main dish servings.

------------------------

948058 -- SHRIMP   SCAMPI

6 cloves garlic
1 1/2 lb. lg. shrimp
1 tbsp. butter
3 tbsp. oil
Salt & pepper
1 tbsp. lemon juice
2 tbsp. chopped fresh parsley

Mince garlic. Shell and devein shrimp, leaving tails on. In large frying pan, melt the butter in the oil over medium high heat. Add shrimp and cook, stirring occasionally until just cooked through, about 5 minutes. Stir in the garlic and cook about 30 seconds. Remove from heat and add 1/2 teaspoon salt, 1/4 teaspoon pepper, lemon juice and parsley. Toss until shrimp are coated. Serve immediately. Note: You may cut down on the amount of garlic used depending on your own like or dislike of a strong garlic flavor. T4544 Records   SDR 11:  Second End Connectors, after forming.

------------------------

948059 -- SQUARE   SHRIMP   FOO   YOUNG

5 beaten eggs
1 (4 oz.) can shrimp
1 chopped onion
1 c. chopped celery
1 can sliced water chestnuts
1/2 c. fresh sliced mushrooms
1 tbsp. soy sauce
2 tbsp. soy sauce
2 tbsp. cornstarch
1 beef bouillon cube
1/4 c. boiling water
1/4 tsp. sugar

Combine eggs, shrimp, onion, celery, chestnuts, mushrooms and 1 tablespoon soy sauce in bowl.  Dissolve bouillon in water.  Add combined 2 tablespoons soy sauce and cornstarch and sugar to the bouillon water over medium low heat and cook until very thick.  Add this sauce to the egg mix.  Heat wok until 300 degrees (or skillet) and pour the mix in spreading evenly.  Cook 10 minutes, cut into squares and turn.  Cook 5 minutes on other side.   T4544 Records

------------------------

### 948060 -- FRIED OYSTERS

Fresh oysters are best, but you can use store bought ones if need be.  Rinse and dry well.  Roll in bread crumbs, then beaten egg.  Then in bread crumbs again.  Fry oysters in butter until brown and well done.  Season with salt, pepper and paprika to taste.

------------------------

### 948061 -- OYSTER BAKE

1 1/2 pt. oysters
3-4 c. cracker crumbs
3/4 lb. melted butter

In 9 x 13 inch baking dish, alternate layers of crackers, oysters and butter.  Bake at 350 degrees for 1 hour.   T4544 Records

------------------------

### 948062 -- DAN'S WHOLE BAKED AND DECORATED SALMON

1 salmon cleaned with head, tail and skin on.  Roll up a lot of foil and place into belly for support.  Stand fish up (like it were swimming) on sheet pan.  Cover fish with salad oil and season with salt and pepper.  To seal completely wrap fish with foil.  To help hold fish up while baking use coffee mugs full of water.  Line pan with diced onions and celery.  Fill pan with water or white wine.  Bake at 275 degrees for 3-4 hours until done, depending on size of fish.  Remove from oven.  Cool overnight or until cold enough to decorate.  Peel off skin on sides leave head, tail as is.  Remove fins.  Carefully trim off grey fat to expose pink meat.  Coat with unflavored gelatin and cool.  Repeat 3-4 coats and then decorate; with lemons, prawns, shrimp, crab legs and tomatoes.  Glaze with gelatin after to hold pieces on .  This is exceptional as a center piece for dinner party, and it tastes great too.   T4541 Test

------------------------

## 948063 -- BATTER FOR FRIED SHRIMP

1 c. flour
1/2 tsp. sugar
1/2 tsp. salt
1 egg
3/4 c. ice water
1/4 c. milk
2 tbsp. vegetable oil

Combine ingredients and beat well. Dip shrimp and fry in deep fat.

------------------------

## 948064 -- SHRIMP SPAGHETTI GRATIN

3 lb. raw shrimp
2 tsp. salt
1 1/2 tbsp. pepper
1/2 tsp. basil
1/2 tsp. thyme
1/4 tsp. garlic powder
1 tsp. prepared barbecue seasoning
1 tbsp. parsley flakes
1 tbsp. lemon juice
1 tbsp. Worcestershire sauce
1 1/2 c. butter, cut in 1" slices
8 oz. spaghetti, cooked & drained
8 oz. Velveeta cheese, grated

Wash the shrimp in cold water and drain them for 1 hour. In a large shallow baking dish arrange the shrimp evenly. Combine the herbs, spices and seasonings; sprinkle mixture over the shrimp. Add the lemon juice, Worcestershire sauce, barbecue seasoning and butter. Bake the mixture, uncovered, at 350 degrees for 25 minutes, stirring occasionally. Peel the shrimp when they are cool enough to handle. (Note: I prefer to peel the shrimp before cooking, it is not as messy.) Transfer the sauce in the bottom of the baking dish to a container with a pouring lip. Arrange the shrimp on the spaghetti and pour sauce over. Top with cheese and bake at 350 degrees until cheese is melted and bubbly.

------------------------

## 948065 -- SHRIMP KABOBS

1 (8 oz.) pkg. frozen peeled &
  deveined shrimp

3 tbsp. soy sauce
2 tbsp. catsup
1/8 tsp. ground ginger
Dash onion powder
1 (8 oz.) can pineapple chunks (juice pack), drained
1/4 c. cashews or peanuts, coarsely chopped (optional)
Hot cooked rice

1. Place frozen shrimp in a colander. Run cool water over shrimp just until thawed. Pat dry with paper towels. 2. Meanwhile, stir together soy sauce, catsup, ginger and onion powder. Set aside. Alternately thread four 12 inch skewers with shrimp and pineapple chunks. Place the skewers on the unheated rack of a broiler pan. Brush with some of the soy mixture. 3. Broil 4 to 5 inches from heat for 2 minutes. Turn kabobs. Brush with more soy mixture. Broil 1-3 minutes more or until shrimp turns pink. Brush with remaining soy mixture. Stir cashews or peanuts into hot cooked rice. Serve kabobs with rice.
Garnish with celery leaves, if desired. Makes 2 servings.

------------------------

## 948066 -- SALMON CROQUETTES

2 c. cooked fresh salmon (or other leftover cooked fish)
2 tbsp. low-fat or fat-free mayonnaise
1/2 c. unseasoned dry bread crumbs, divided

1/4 c. finely chopped scallions, divided
2 tbsp. minced parsley, divided
Freshly ground black pepper
Few dashes red pepper sauce
1 egg white, beaten until foamy
1 c. canned crushed tomatoes
Salt to taste
Lemon & parsley for garnish

Coarsely chop salmon and place in medium bowl. Mix with mayonnaise, 1/4 cup of the bread crumbs, 2 tablespoons of the scallions, 1 tablespoon of the parsley, black pepper and hot sauce. Stir in egg white. Shape into 4 patties and coat lightly with remaining bread crumbs. Cover and refrigerate. In small nonstick skillet combine tomatoes and remaining scallions; simmer about 10 minutes. Stir in remaining parsley, season with salt and pepper. Keep sauce warm. Place croquettes on foil-lined broiler pan. Broil 4-6 inches from heat source until lightly browned (about 4-5 minutes per side). To serve: Place 1/4 cup sauce on each individual plate, top with 2 salmon croquettes and garnish with lemon wedge and parsley. Serves 2.

------------------------

## 948067 -- MICHAELS MARVELOUS MUSSELS

Cook in a heavy skillet: 2 lg. cloves garlic, chopped
2 tbsp. olive oil
1 bag mussels
1/2 c. wine

Wash and clean mussels. Brown garlic in olive oil; add wine and mussels. Simmer covered until mussels steam open. Do not drain. Serve with Italian bread.

------------------------

## 948068 -- BARBECUED SHRIMP

1 c. butter (2 sticks)
1 (16 oz.) bottle Italian dressing
4 tbsp. minced garlic
2 tbsp. Worcestershire sauce
2 tbsp. black pepper
2 tsp. lemon juice
2 lb. large fresh, unshelled shrimp
1 lg. lemon, thinly sliced
Sliced French bread

Place butter, dressing, garlic, Worcestershire sauce, pepper and lemon juice in a large skillet or saucepan. Cook over medium heat until butter melts. Turn off heat and let stand for 20 minutes. Place shrimp in a large baking pan. Pour sauce over shrimp and stir lightly. Cover all shrimp with sauce. Place lemon slice over shrimp. Bake in a preheated 400 degree oven for 15 to 20 minutes or until shrimp turn pink. Do not overcook or shrimp will dry out. Serve with bread for dipping.

------------------------

## 948069 -- SALMON PATTIES

2 lg. eggs
2 (7 1/2 oz. each) cans red sockeye
    salmon, drained, flaked
2/3 c. fine dry bread crumbs
1/2 c. finely chopped onion

1/4 c. finely chopped parsley
1 to 2 tbsp. lemon juice
1/4 tsp. salt
Pepper to taste
1 c. corn oil

In medium bowl, beat eggs enough to blend yolks and whites; stir in salmon, 1/3 cup of the bread crumbs, onion, parsley, lemon juice, salt and pepper until well-mixed. Shape into 4 (each about 1" thick) oval-shaped patties. Coat with remaining bread crumbs. Line a tray with wax paper and place the patties, well apart and refrigerate at least 30 minutes. In a 10 inch skillet over medium heat, heat oil. Add patties. Shallow - fry, turning once, until evenly browned. Drain on paper towels. Serve very hot. Good accompanied with tartar sauce.

------------------------

## 948070 -- SHRIMP DE JONGHE

2 cloves garlic, mash to a paste, mix with 1/3 teaspoon tarragon, parsley, chervil shallot. Add to 1/2 cup sweet butter and 1 cup bread crumbs blended together. Season to taste with dash salt, pepper, nutmeg, mace and thyme. Add 1/2 cup dry sherry. Alternate layers of 2 pounds shelled and deveined cooked shrimp with above mixture. Top with generously buttered bread crumbs. Bake at 400 degrees for 15-20 minutes.

------------------------

## 948071 -- SHRIMP SCAMPI

6 cloves garlic, minced
1 1/2 lb. lg. jumbo shrimp, shelled
    and deveined, leave tails on
1 tbsp. butter
3 tbsp. oil
1/2 tsp. salt
1/4 tsp. pepper
1 tbsp. lemon juice
2 tbsp. chopped fresh parsley

Melt butter in oil. Add shrimps. Cook about 5 minutes. Stir in garlic, cook 30 seconds. Remove from heat. Add salt, pepper, lemon juice, and parsley. Toss until coated. Serve immediately.

------------------------

## 948072 -- POOR-MAN'S LOBSTER

Water in Dutch oven
1 unpeeled potato
1 whole onion, skinless
2 lb. fish
1 tbsp. salt
2 tbsp. lemon juice

Boil water, potato, onion, salt, and lemon juice for 45 minutes. Put frozen fish in and boil for 15 minutes or until flakes apart. Serve with a stick of melted butter and 2 dashes Tabasco sauce and lemon, or with tartar sauce.

------------------------

948073 -- SALMON   PATTIES

2 sm. cans salmon
1/4 c. chopped onion
2 tbsp. butter
2/3 c. bread crumbs or crackers
2 eggs, beaten
1 tsp. parsley
1 tsp. dry mustard

Brown onion in butter. Drain salmon, reserve 1/3 cup of liquid. Remove any bones. Mix into browned onion the salmon, 1/3 cup salmon liquid, egg, parsley, mustard and 1/3 cup crumbs. Shape into patties, roll in remaining 1/3 cup crumbs. Fry until lightly browned. 8 patties.

------------------------

948074 -- SIMPLE   SALMON

1 lg. can red salmon
1/4 c. onion, chopped fine
1 or 2 tbsp. vinegar
Salt and pepper to taste

Remove bones from salmon. Mix all ingredients well. Cover and chill a few hours to blend flavors. Serve on fresh homemade bread or crackers.

------------------------

948075 -- CRAB   SALAD

1 lb. imitation crab meat, cut in bite

size pieces
1 to 2 stalks celery, chopped fine
Mayonnaise to taste

Combine all ingredients and serve on lettuce leaf or on a croissant for a great sandwich.

------------------------

## 948076 -- BARBEQUED SHRIMP

3 slices bacon, chopped
1/2 lb. margarine
2 tbsp. Dijon style mustard
1 1/2 tsp. chili powder
1/4 tsp. basil
1/4 tsp. thyme
1 tsp. coarse black pepper
1/2 tsp. oregano
2 cloves garlic, crushed
2 tbsp. crab boil
1/2 tsp. Tabasco sauce
1 1/2 lb. lg. shrimp, with shells

Preheat oven to 375 degrees. In a small frying pan fry bacon until clear; add margarine and all other ingredients except the shrimp. Simmer for 5 minutes. Place the shrimp in an open baking dish, and pour sauce over the top. Stir once to coat all the shrimp. Bake in an uncovered dish for 20 minutes, stirring twice during the baking process. Serve hot and at once! You may peel these shrimp before eating, but not before cooking. Have a towel ready for each guest, for this most delicious dish is very messy!!

------------------------

## 948077 -- CRAB SHRIMP MORAY

1 stick butter
1/2 c. flour
1/4 c. grated onion
1/2 c. chopped green onion
1/8 c. chopped parsley
2 c. cream
1 c. dry white wine or vermouth
2 1/2 tsp. salt
1/2 tsp. white pepper
1/4 tsp. cayenne pepper

2 1/2 oz. Grugere imported Swiss
   cheese
2 cans artichokes (bottoms quartered)
2 tbsp. lemon juice
2 lb. shrimp
1 lb. lump crab meat
1/2 lb. sliced fresh mushrooms
3 tbsp. grated Romano cheese

In a 2 quart sauce pan melt butter, stir in flour and cook 5 minutes over medium flames, stirring. Add onions, green onions and cook 2 to 3 minutes, stirring. Add parsley and gradually add cream. Allow to get hot but do not boil. Add wine, salt and peppers. Blend well and bring to a simmer, stirring occasionally. Add Swiss cheese, cover, turn off heat and cool. When lukewarm add lemon juice. In a 3 quart casserole make alternate layers of crab meat, shrimp, quartered artichoke bottoms, sliced raw mushrooms, using sauce between layers and on top. Cover and refrigerate until ready to reheat for serving. Pur uncovered, room temperature casserole in a 350 degree oven for 30 to 45 minutes. Before baking sprinkle with Romano cheese. Serve in pastry cups. Serves 8 to 10.

------------------------

### 948078 -- ROYAL   SEAFOOD   CASSEROLE

2 cans cream of shrimp soup
1/2 c. mayonnaise
1 sm. onion, grated
3/4 c. milk
Salt and pepper (cayenne)
Worcestershire sauce
Lemon juice to taste
3 lb. shrimp (cleaned and boiled)
1 can (5 oz.) crab meat (rinsed and
   drained)
1 can water chestnuts, drained and
   sliced
3/4 c. diced celery
1/4 c. diced bell pepper
1 1/2 c. uncooked rice (cook and cool)
Paprika and sliced almonds for garnish

Blend together soup and mayonnaise, add remaining ingredients. If mixture is dry, additional milk may be added. Bake at 350 degrees for 30 minutes. Serves 4 to 5.

------------------------

## 948079 -- SALMON

1 can salmon
1/2 c. meal
1 egg

Mix all ingredients together. With 2 teaspoons, scoop mixture with one, push off with other. Put into deep hot fat. When fried, they will float and turn themselves.

------------------------

## 948080 -- HOT BUTTERED SHRIMP

Cleaned, boiled shrimp
1 bottle Italian dressing
1 stick butter
Juice of 1 lemon

Combine last 3 ingredients and simmer shrimp in sauce for at least 15 minutes before serving.

------------------------

## 948081 -- LOW COUNTRY SHRIMP BOIL

4 qts. water
2 bottles beer (optional)
2 lemons, quartered
2 onions, quartered

1 (2 oz.) Special Seasoning (I use
   Old Bay)
2 bay leaves
2 potatoes, quartered
1 Hillshire Farm Polska Kielbasa, cut
   in chunks
1 pkg. Sweet Select Corn on the cob
1 1/2 - 2 lb. shrimp, head off-shells
   on

Combine first 6 ingredients, cook at a rolling boil for 15 minutes. Lower to medium boil; add sausage. Cook 15-20 minutes, then add potatoes, cook 15-20 minutes, then add corn. Cook 15-20 minutes. Bring back to a rolling boil; add shrimp. Cook 1-3 minutes. Drain and serve. Serves 4.

------------------------

## 948082 -- SHRIMP AND PASTA

1 lb. shrimp, cleaned, cooked &
   deveined
1 lb. rotini, cooked
1 c. broccoli & cauliflower, flowerets
1/4 c. green onions
1 sm. jar pimiento, drained
1/8 c. mayonnaise
1/8 c. sour cream
1/4 c. thousand island salad dressing
2 tbsp. lemon juice
Salt, white pepper & red pepper to
   taste

  Mix mayonnaise, sour cream, salad dressing, lemon juice, salt and peppers.  Combine with remaining ingredients.  Refrigerate 4 hours before serving.

------------------------

## 948083 -- SPICY BAKED SHRIMP

1/2 c. olive oil
2 tbsp. cajun or creole seasoning
2 tbsp. fresh lemon juice
2 tbsp. chopped fresh parsley
1 tbsp. honey
1 tbsp. soy sauce
Pinch of cayenne pepper
1 lb. uncooked large shrimp, shelled,
   deveined

  Combine first 7 ingredients in 9x13 inch baking dish.  Add shrimp and toss to coat.  Refrigerate one hour.  Bake at 450 degrees for about 10 minutes, stirring occasionally.  Serves 4.   LL - Teacher

------------------------

## 948084 -- SPICY SHRIMP

1/2 c. olive oil
2 tbsp. cajun seasoning
2 tbsp. fresh lemon juice
2 tbsp. chopped fresh parsley
1 tbsp. honey

1 tbsp. soy sauce
Pinch cayenne pepper
1 lb. shrimp, shelled & deveined
1 pkg. fresh linguini or angel hair
    pasta & prepare as directed

Combine first 7 ingredients in 9x13 inch baking dish. Add shrimp and toss to coat. Refrigerate one hour. Preheat oven to 450 degrees. Bake until shrimp are cooked thoroughly, stirring occasionally, about 10 minutes. Serve over pasta. Garnish with lemon wedge and serve with French bread.

------------------------

### 948085 -- LEMON & GARLIC SHRIMP

1 1/2 lb. lg. shrimp (in shell)
2 cloves garlic
1 scallion
1 lemon
1 tbsp. butter
2 tbsp. olive oil
Salt
2 tbsp. chopped fresh parsley

Peel and devein shrimp. Mince the garlic and chop scallion. Squeeze 2 tablespoons juice from lemon. Heat butter and oil in a large frying pan over medium heat. Add the shrimp, garlic and 1 teaspoon salt. Saute, stirring until shrimp turns pink (3-4 minutes). Stir in lemon juice and scallions. Sprinkle with parsley and serve. 4 servings.

------------------------

### 948086 -- POOR MAN'S LOBSTER

2 c. water
1 tbsp. vinegar
1 tbsp. Old Bay seasoning
1 tsp. celery seed
Salt
1 lb. frozen haddock

Bring all ingredients to a boil then add haddock. Cook 25 minutes. Serve with hot melted butter.

------------------------

### 948087 -- SPAGHETTI & SHRIMP SALAD

8 oz. very thin spaghetti
1 cucumber, seeded & chopped
1 bunch radishes, sliced
1 bunch scallions, including 1 inch
   of green tops, sliced
1 lb. med. shrimp, cleaned & cooked,
   chopped in pieces

--DRESSING:--

1 c. mayonnaise
1/3 c. milk
1/3 c. bottled cole slaw dressing
2 tsp. Dijon mustard
1 tbsp. red wine vinegar
Juice of 1 lemon
1 tsp. salt
1/2 tsp. sugar
1/2 tsp. freshly ground pepper
1/2 tsp. celery salt
1/8 tsp. basil
1 tbsp. dried parsley

Break spaghetti into quarters. Cook according to package directions with 1 tablespoon oil. Drain. Add remaining ingredients. DRESSING: Combine dressing ingredients. Toss dressing and spaghetti mixture and refrigerate several hours or overnight. 8 servings.

-----------------------

948088 -- BOW TIES WITH SHRIMP AND BROCCOLI

1 head fresh broccoli
1 lb. med. shrimp
1 can chicken broth
1 med. onion, finely sliced
1 lg. tomato, diced
1/3 c. olive oil
1 lb. bow tie macaroni, cooked
   according to pkg. directions

Wash and cut up fresh broccoli. Simmer broccoli in 1 can chicken broth until tender. Heat oil in skillet. Saute' onion and shrimp until pink. Add diced tomato and broccoli and broth. Pour over cooked pasta. Serve immediately. Sprinkle with grated cheese.

------------------------

948089 -- SHRIMP   SALAD   CRUNCH

1 can shrimp
1 c. cut up celery
1 c. slivered raw carrots
1 tsp. diced onion
1 c. mayonnaise
1 sm. can shoe string potatoes

Combine all ingredients just before serving.

------------------------

948090 -- NEW   ENGLAND   SEAFOOD   CHOWDER

1 lb. whitefish, skin and bones removed
1 c. diced celery
1 lg. onion, chopped
5 med. potatoes, peeled and cubed
3 tbsp. all-purpose flour
1/3 c. cold water
2 cans (6-1/2 oz. each) minced clams,
   liquid reserved
1 can (4 oz.) tiny shrimp, drained
2 tsp. salt
1/2 tsp. pepper
2 tbsp. butter or margarine
1 can (12 oz.) evaporated milk
1/2 jar (1 oz.) pimiento, drained
Fresh chopped parsley

In a large Dutch oven, place fish and enough water to cover.  Cook over medium heat until fish flakes with a fork, about 10 minutes.  With a slotted spoon, remove fish and break into bite-size pieces; set aside.  Measure cooking liquid and add enough additional water to equal 4 cups.  In the liquid, cook celery, onions and potatoes until tender.  Combine the flour and water to make a paste;  stir into chowder.  Cook and stir until mixture boils. Add reserved fish, clams with liquid, shrimp, crabmeat, salt, pepper, butter, milk and pimiento. Heat through, stirring occasionally. Garnish with parsley.  Yields:  3-1/2 quarts.  I don't lawn of a recipe that better represents our area than chowder.  I adapted it from my mom's clam chowder recipe, and guests often request it.

------------------------

## 948091 -- LAYERED CRAB SALAD

4 c. torn lettuce
2 c. (1/2 lb.) fresh pea pods, cut
   into 1-inch pieces
1 1/2 c. chopped red peppers
2 c. chopped cucumber
1 1/2 c. crabmeat or 1 pkg. (8 oz.)
   imitation crabmeat
1 c. mayonnaise
1 tbsp. sugar
1 tsp. dried dill weed or 1 tbsp.
   chopped fresh dill
Sweet red pepper rings
Fresh dill sprigs

In a 2-1/2 quart clear glass serving bowl, layer lettuce, pea pods, chopped peppers, cucumber and crabmeat. Combine mayonnaise, sugar and dill; spread over crab. Cover and chill several hours or overnight. Garnish with pepper rings and dill. Yield: 6 servings. I am secretary of the University of Oregon. I love living in Oregon and enjoy cooking with the many foods available in this part of the country. Crabmeat is abundant here and makes a great company dinner.

------------------------

## 948092 -- CRAB SOUP

1/4 c. margarine
1/4 c. celery, chopped
1/4 c. flour
6 to 10 drops hot pepper sauce
5 c. skim milk
16 oz. flaked imitation crab meat (3
   1/2 c.)
1/4 c. scallions, sliced

Melt margarine in large saucepan. Add celery, cook 3 minutes. Add flour and stir over low heat until frothy. Cook additional 3 minutes, stirring often. Add hot pepper sauce. Gradually stir in milk. Increase heat and bring to a boil, then reduce heat to simmer. Allow to simmer and thicken 10 minutes. Add crab meat and scallions. Makes 4 servings.

------------------------

## 948093 -- SEAFOOD SALAD

1 (7 oz.) pkg. macaroni rings
6 to 8 seafood legs, cut in pieces
1 lg. onion, finely chopped
2 stalks celery, finely chopped
3 or 4 lg. cauliflowerets, thinly sliced
Frozen peas, thawed (optional)
1 c. Spin Blend (more if desired)
1/2 c. cottage cheese (more if desired)
Salt & pepper to taste

Cook macaroni as directed on package; drain. Mix gently with seafood logs, onion, celery, cauliflower, and peas. Combine Spin Blend and cottage cheese; carefully stir into macaroni mixture. Add salt and pepper. Makes 8 to 10 servings. Chill immediately.

------------------------

948094 -- CRAB GUMBO

2 onions
4 tomatoes
7 c. water
10 okra
2 bay leaves
3 sprigs parsley
1 1/2 tsp. salt
1/2 tsp. thyme
1/4 tsp. chili peppers
4 tbsp. butter
1 lb. lump crabmeat

Add all ingredients together except crabmeat and butter. Cook for 30 minutes. Cook crabmeat and butter together for 20 minutes. Add together and cook over low heat for 30 minutes.

------------------------

948095 -- SHRIMP BISQUE

1 lb. shrimp, boiled, peeled & finely chopped
1/2 c. chopped yellow onion
1/2 c. chopped celery

4 tbsp. butter
4 tbsp. flour
4 c. fish stock
1 tsp. salt
1/4 tsp. white pepper
1/8 tsp. hot pepper sauce
2 c. whipping cream

Make this a day before serving and do not freeze it. Saute chopped onion and celery in butter for 4 minutes. Sprinkle flour over vegetables and quickly stir to form an even coating for about 2 minutes. Stir in hot fish stock and bring to a boil. Reduce heat and simmer 15 minutes. Add cooked shrimp and continue stirring for 10 to 15 minutes. Add salt, pepper and hot pepper sauce. Right before serving reheat soup and add cream. Gently heat through. Do not boil!
Serve immediately. Serves 8.

------------------------

948096 -- SHRIMP & RICE SALAD

1 c. uncooked rice
6 scallions, sliced
1 lb. shrimp, cooked & peeled
1 c. (homemade) mayonnaise
1/2 tsp. ground ginger
Juice of 1 lemon
Salt to taste
Toasted sesame seeds
Steamed snow peas

Cook rice and let cool. Add scallions, shrimp, mayonnaise, ginger, lemon juice and salt. Adjust seasonings to taste. Cool in refrigerator several hours if desired. Serve at room temperature, sprinkled with sesame seeds and surrounded by snow peas on a large platter or shallow bowl. Serves 6.

------------------------

948097 -- SANTA FE SHRIMP SALAD

--DRESSING:--

4 sm. green onions, chopped
1 c. chopped fresh cilantro
1 c. fresh lime juice
2 tbsp. olive oil
1 tbsp. sugar

1/4 jalapeno chili, chopped sm.
1 tsp. salt

--SALAD:--

1 1/2 c. frozen corn, thawed
1 (15 oz.) can black beans, rinsed
1 med. zucchini, diced
1 avocado, peeled, diced
1 lg. red bell pepper, diced
3/4 c. diced red onion
1 1/4 lbs. lg. peeled, deveined
   cooked shrimp
Red leaf lettuce

Blend dressing ingredients in blender or food processor until smooth. I cook shrimp after peeling and deveining them by pan frying them for a few minutes in Italian dressing. Combine corn, black beans, zucchini, avocado, red pepper and red onion in large bowl. Reserve 6 or more shrimp for garnish. Cut remaining shrimp crosswise into 1/2 inch thick rounds, add to salad. Toss salad with dressing. Cover and refrigerate for at least 1 hour. Arrange lettuce leaves on plates or in a large dish. Top with salad. Garnish with whole shrimp, cilantro sprigs and lime wedges.

------------------------

948098 -- SALMON PASTA SALAD WITH SAN FRANCISCO VINAIGRETTE

--SALMON PASTA SALAD:--

1 green bell pepper, seeded, washed &
   minced
1 red bell pepper, seeded, washed &
   minced
1 bunch celery stalks, minced
1 bunch fresh dill, minced or 2 tsp.
   dried
2 tsp. olive oil
3 c. mayonnaise
1/4 c. Dijon mustard
Salt & pepper to taste
1 (15 1/2 oz.) can salmon, drained &
   flaked
2 lbs. shell pasta, cooked al dente
1 1/2 c. San Francisco Vinaigrette,
   recipe below
1 c. fresh Parmesan cheese, grated or

use shaker style
Green pepper, mushrooms, cherry
   tomatoes or avocados or any
   combination thereof for garnish

In a large bowl place the minced green and red peppers, celery, dill, olive oil, mayonnaise, mustard, salt and pepper. Mix the ingredients together. Add the salmon and mix it in. Add the pasta and mix it in. Add the Vinaigrette and mix the ingredients together thoroughly. Adjust seasonings if necessary.
Sprinkle with the Parmesan and garnish. Serves at least 10.

--SAN FRANCISCO VINAIGRETTE--

2 cloves garlic, chopped
1/4 red bell pepper, seeded, washed &
   chopped
1 tsp. thyme
1/2 c. red wine vinegar (or mix 1/2 &
   1/2 with balsamic vinegar)
2 tsp. Dijon mustard
1 c. olive oil
1 tsp. sugar
1 tsp. salt
1 tsp. pepper

Mix all ingredients except the oil together. Add oil in a steady stream while using a wire whisk or fork until desired consistency is achieved. Cover and refrigerate.

------------------------

948099 -- CRAB   SALAD

1 loaf white sandwich bread, sliced
2 cans crab, drained
1 can tiny shrimp
About 3 c. mayonnaise
4 hard-boiled eggs
1 sm. onion, chopped
1 c. celery, chopped

Freeze the bread. This makes it easier to cut. Butter the bread, trim off crusts and cube. Ad 4 hard boiled eggs and the onion; mix well and refrigerate overnight. Four hours before serving, add the crab, shrimp and one cup chopped celery and enough mayonnaise to moisten. This makes a large salad. Would serve 10 to 12.

------------------------

## 948100 -- SHRIMP SALAD WITH BROWN RICE

1 c. brown rice
1 1/2 c. fresh shrimp
1/2 c. celery, cut up
1/2 c. mayonnaise
1 tsp. curry powder
1/2 c. green onion, chopped
Salt & pepper to taste
Paprika

Cook rice and when done let cool well. Add remaining ingredients and mix. Garnish with paprika.

------------------------

## 948101 -- SHRIMP SALAD

1 c. carrots, shredded
1/2 c. grated sharp cheese
1/2 c. mayonnaise
1 c. celery, chopped
1/4 c. onion, chopped
1 c. shrimp, drained

Let all combined stand in refrigerator at least 3 hours. Before serving add 1 can of chow mein noodles.

------------------------

## 948102 -- SEAFOOD WILD RICE

--DRESSING:--

1 tbsp. garlic, minced
2 tbsp. curry powder
1/4 c. olive oil
2 c. mayonnaise
1/2 tsp. salt & pepper
2 tbsp. sugar
1/2 c. orange juice
1/4 c. lemon juice
1/4 c. chutney, chopped

--WILD RICE:--

1 lb. wild rice, uncooked
5 c. chicken broth
1 1/4 c. frozen petite peas
3/4 c. celery, diced
1/2 c. green onion, chopped
1 lb. sm. to med. shrimp, cooked,
   peeled & deveined
1 lb. sea legs or crab meat, cut in
   1/2 pieces

Saute garlic and curry in olive oil in small skillet. Combine remaining dressing ingredients in medium bowl. Mix well. Add garlic mixture. Simmer rice in chicken broth one hour, until rice is tender and puffed open. Drain and cool. Add remaining ingredients; toss with dressing. Rochester, MN

------------------------

948103 -- SALMON   STEW

1 can pink salmon
2 med. onions, chopped
1 can tomato soup
2 c. boiled potatoes
Dash of Tabasco sauce

Make sure you pick all the little bones out of salmon. Put in large pot and add chopped onions, soup and chopped, boiled potatoes and Tabasco sauce. Simmer about 20 minutes. Serve over a bed of rice.

------------------------

948105 -- SHRIMP   SALAD

1 pkg. salad macaroni, cooked
1 ($5.00) bag shrimp, cooked & chopped
1 c. celery, chopped
1 med. onion, chopped
1 green pepper, chopped

Mix all together and salt to taste. --DRESSING:--

About 1 c. mayonnaise
1 tbsp. sugar
Scant tsp. vinegar cut with little
   water

Mix and toss with salad ingredients.   Tampa Bay, Florida

------------------------

## 948107 -- SHRIMP   MACARONI   SALAD

1/3 c. corn oil
1 lb. med. shrimp, shelled and
   deveined
2 cloves garlic
1/4 c. white wine
2 tsp. Dijon mustard
2 tbsp. vinegar
1 tsp. salt
f.g. pepper
8 oz. sm. pasta shells, cooked
1 can artichoke hearts, drained and
   quartered
1/2 c. red pepper, thinly sliced
1/2 c. black olives, sliced
1/2 c. onions, minced

In a large skillet heat oil over a medium high heat.  Add shrimp and garlic and saute until shrimp is pink.  Remove from heat.  Stir in wine, vinegar, mustard, salt and pepper.  In a large bowl combine shrimp, pasta, artichokes, peppers, olives and onions.  Toss gently to coat.  Cover and chill for 1 hour.

------------------------

## 948108 -- SEAFOOD   CHOWDER

1 c. chopped onion
1/2 c. sliced celery
1 garlic clove
2 (16 oz.) can stewed tomatoes
1/2 c. white wine
1/2 c. parsley
1/4 tsp. thyme
1/4 tsp. pepper
1 lb. fish - use firm fish such as
   shark, halibut, swordfish
2 cans tiny shrimp

Saute onion, celery, garlic in olive oil.  Add tomatoes, wine, parsley, thyme,  pepper.  Simmer 20 minutes.  Add fish and shrimp.  Simmer 7 to 10 minutes.

------------------------

### 948109 -- SEAFOOD SALAD

4 to 5 c. crab meat  
1 c. green pepper, chopped  
1 c. onion, chopped  
2 tbsp. vinegar  
1 tsp. salt  
1 c. celery, chopped  
As much chopped lettuce as desired  

Mix all ingredients well and refrigerate.

------------------------

### 948110 -- MACARONI AND SHRIMP SALAD

12 oz. pkg. Elbow macaroni  
2 c. frozen peas, thawed and drained  
6 hard boiled eggs  
12 oz. shrimp, or crabmeat  
4 green onions, diced  
2 carrots, grated  
1 green pepper, diced  
1 3/4 c. celery, chopped  
Spices: salt, pepper, a little  
   seasoned salt, garlic powder and  
   dried parsley.  
Mayonnaise, probably 2 c. or so  

Mix all ingredients together.

------------------------

### 948111 -- SEAFOOD SALAD

1/2 lb. imitation crab  
2 hard boiled eggs, chopped  
1/4 c. chopped celery  
1 tbsp. minced dried chives  
1/2 c. mayonnaise  
1 tsp. prepared mustard  
1 tbsp. chopped dill pickles  
1 tsp. salt

1 tsp. lemon juice
1/4 tsp. pepper

Combine and chill.   Serves 4.   Recipe can be doubled and tripled.

------------------------

### 948112 -- CRAB   BISQUE

1 can mushroom soup
1 can asparagus soup
1 1/2 cans evaporated milk
1/2 lb. crab meat
1 c. half and half
1/4 c. cooking sherry option
1 tsp. old bay seasoning

Blend soups and stir in milk and cream.   Heat to boiling.   Add crab meat and heat.

------------------------

### 948113 -- CREAM   OF   CRAB   SOUP

1 can cream of asparagus soup
1 can cream of mushroom soup
1 can cream of celery soup
3 cans of milk
1 lb. crab meat
Parsley flakes
Old bay seasoning

Bring soup and milk to simmer.   Add crab meat and simmer for 30 minutes.   Add old bay to taste.   Serve hot.

------------------------

### 948114 -- CORN   AND   CRAB   BISQUE

1/2 c. chop celery
1/2 c. chopped green onions
1/4 c. chopped green pepper
1/2 c. butter, melted
2 cans of potato soup
1 can cream corn
1 1/2 c. half and half
1 1/2 c. milk

2 bay leaves
1 tsp. dried thyme
1/2 tsp. garlic powder
1/4 tsp. white pepper
Dash hot sauce
1 lb. crabmeat
Chop parsley and lemon slices,
   optional

Saute' celery, green pepper and onions in butter, in Dutch oven.  Add soup, corn, half and half, milk, bay leaves, thyme, garlic powder, pepper and hot sauce; cook until thoroughly heated.  Gently stir in crab meat and heat.  Discard bay leaves.  Garnish with parsley and lemon slices if desired.  Yield:  11 cups.

------------------------

948115 -- MACARONI   AND   SALMON   SALAD

1 lb. elbow macaroni
1 (14 oz.) can salmon or 2 cans tuna
6 tbsp. mayonnaise
1 tsp. mustard
3 sm. onions

Boil macaroni for about 12 to 15 minutes or until cooked.  Drain and rinse.  Drain juice from canned salmon.  ????  Crumble into small pieces.  Mix mayonnaise, mustard, and onions into macaroni.  Mix well and refrigerate.

------------------------

948116 -- EGG   &   SMOKED   SALMON   SALAD

12 lg. eggs, hard-cooked, shelled &
   coarsely chopped
2 ribs celery, chopped
1 sm. red onion, minced
3 tbsp. fresh dill, chopped
5 oz. smoked salmon, cut into 1/4
   inch, diced
1 c. (or as needed) Hellmann's light
   mayonnaise
Salt & freshly ground pepper to taste

Place the eggs, celery, onion, dill and salmon in a mixing bowl and toss to combine.  Stir in enough mayonnaise to bind the salad, being careful not to make it too wet.  Season to taste with salt and pepper.  Refrigerate for several hours to allow the flavors to blend.

------------------------

## 948117 -- CRAB & CORN BISQUE

1/2 c. green onions
1/2 c. celery, chopped
1/4 c. green pepper, chopped
1/2 c. butter, melted

Saute above ingredients in large pan.

--ADD ADDITIONAL INGREDIENTS:--

2 cans cream of potato soup
2 cans creamed corn
3 c. milk
2 bay leaves
1 tsp. thyme
1/4 tsp. pepper
Dash of hot sauce

Cook until heated.  Stir in 1 pound crabmeat and discard the bay leaves.  Makes 10 cups.

------------------------

## 948118 -- SHRIMP - VEGETABLE BISQUE

3 1/2 c. (about 1 lb.) zucchini, sliced
1 c. carrots, sliced
1/2 c. celery, chopped
1/2 c. green onion, sliced
1/2 c. butter
1 tbsp. flour
1 3/4 c. milk
2 c. water
1 can cream of mushroom soup
1/2 c. dry white wine (or increase
    water by 1/2 c.)
1/2 c. sour cream
2 tsp. chicken bouillon granules
1 (4 1/2 oz.) can tiny shrimp

In covered Dutch oven, cook zucchini, carrots, celery and onion in butter until tender, about 20 minutes.  Blend in flour.  Stir in milk.  Cook and stir until bubbly.  Pour into blender, cover and blend until smooth.  In same pan combine water, soup, wine, sour cream and bouillon granules. Then stir in the puree and shrimp.  Heat through, but DO NOT BOIL.  Garnish with cucumber slices.  Makes 8 (1 cup) servings.

------------------------

948119 -- SHRIMP   SALAD

2 carrots
2 avocados
1 lb. peeled & cooked lg. shrimp
About 1/3 c. bottled Dijon or mustard
    dressing
Red leaf lettuce leaves for garnish

Using vegetable peeler, draw peeler lengthwise along carrots forming long ribbons. Lengthwise cut avocados in half; remove and discard seeds.  Peel off skin.  Crosswise slice 3/4 of an avocado half and fan into individual serving  plate; chop remaining avocado.  Repeat with remaining avocado halves.  Place chopped avocado in medium bowl with shrimp, carrot ribbons and 1/3 cup dressing; toss until mixture is well coated. Divide and spoon shrimp mixture onto serving plates.  Arrange a few lettuce leaves on plates.  Just before serving, drizzle each serving with a little more dressing.

------------------------

948120 -- SALMON   OR   CLAM   CHOWDER

2 cans of salmon or clams, drain and
    save liquid
4 carrots, diced
3 stalks celery, diced
3 c. diced potatoes
1/2 tsp. thyme
1 bay leaf
1/2 c. butter
2/3 c. onion
4 tbsp. flour
1 tsp. salt
4 c. milk
2 c. shredded cheese, sharp

Melt butter, saute onions, stir in flour until golden brown.  Remove from heat and stir in liquid.  Add celery, potatoes, carrots and add just enough water to cover vegetables. Cook until tender.  Then add milk and cheese, salmon or clams.  Warm (do not boil as milk a will curdle), sprinkle with paprika and serve.

### 948121 -- CRAB BISQUE

1 (10 1/2 oz.) can cream of mushroom
   soup
1 (10 1/2 oz.) can cream of asparagus
   soup
1 1/2 cans milk
1 c. light cream
1 c. crab meat
1/4 c. dry white wine

Blend, heat. Serve with dollop of batter.

---

### 948122 -- SALMON AND SPINACH SOUP

2 c. cooked salmon
2 cloves, pressed garlic
1 med. onion, minced
1 tsp. oregano, crumbled
1/4 tsp. ground nutmeg
1/4 tsp. black pepper
1 tbsp. butter
1 tbsp. olive oil
1 pkg. (10 oz.) frozen chopped
   spinach, thawed undrained
1 bottle (8 oz.) clam juice
2 cans (14 1/2 oz.) chicken broth

In a Dutch oven saute' garlic, onion, oregano, nutmeg, pepper with butter and oil until onion is soft. Add undrained spinach, cook 5 minutes. Pour clam juice into a blender. Spoon in 1/2 sauteed spinach mixture and 1/4 salmon.
Whip until pureed. Pour back into Dutch oven. Add chicken broth and the rest of the salmon, chunked. Simmer 5 minutes.

---

### 948123 -- CRAB SALAD

8 oz. shell macaroni
2 green onions
1/4 lb. snow peas

2 oz. Cheddar cheese
3/4 lb. imitation crab meat
1/4 tsp. salt
1/8 tsp. black pepper
1/8 tsp. onion powder
1/8 tsp. garlic powder
Dash red wine vinegar
1/4 tsp. sugar
1 c. mayonnaise

Cook the shell macaroni until tender. Drain, rinse and cool. Chop the green onions and halve the snow peas. Grate the cheese and shred the crab meat. Mix the onions, snow peas and cheese with the macaroni. Stir in the spices and mix well. Add the mayonnaise and chill until serving time. This make a light and delicious summer meal, if served with bread or rolls and fresh fruit. Serves 4 (as main dish).

------------------------

948124 -- SHRIMP   SALAD

1 pkg. Arzo - 47 (pasta)
1 or 2 lbs. of pre-cooked shrimp
Mayonnaise

Cook pasta as directed on box. Mix cooked pasta and shrimp in large salad bowl. Then take 5 or 6 heaping tablespoons of mayonnaise or to desired smoothness. Then serve as an appetizer or as part of regular dinner. Cornwall,
NY

------------------------

948125 -- SHRIMP   AND   MUSHROOM   CHOWDER

Preparation Time: 30 minutes. Fresh mushrooms and shrimp are the main attractions in this creamy soup. It is ideal to serve on a chilly day for lunch with fresh, hot rolls or bread, as a first course to an elegant meal, or as a late night supper. It can be made ahead and reheated for serving. For 4 servings you will need: 1/2 lb. tiny cooked shrimp, fresh or    frozen
1/2 lb. fresh mushrooms, sliced
1 med. onion, chopped
2 tbsp. butter or margarine
1/4 c. all-purpose flour
2 c. fish broth, clam juice or
   chicken stock
1/2 c. dry white wine (optional)
1/4 to 1/2 tsp. salt

1/2 tsp. dried thyme leaves
1/2 tsp. dill weed
1/4 tsp. mace or nutmeg
1/2 c. whipping cream

TIPS: For the fish broth, save liquid in which you have poached fish. Freeze in 1 cup batches and use for this soup. PREPARATION: Purchase cleaned, shelled shrimp, or rinse frozen shrimp under cold water to remove frost. Drain well. Saute mushrooms and onion in butter for 2 minutes or until onion is tender. Stir in flour. Cook 1 minute more over medium heat. Stir in the broth, juice or stock. Add the wine, if used, and bring to a boil. Add salt, thyme, dill weed and mace or nutmeg. Mix well. Add shrimp. Cook until heated through. Stir in cream just before serving. Heat, but do not boil. Garnish soup if desired, with a few thin slices of uncooked mushroom and a small sprig of fresh parsley or dill, if available. Good served with: Hot French bread or rolls.
For 2 servings: Half of the ingredients. For 8 servings: Double the ingredients but use only 3 1/2 cups broth. Carmel, NY

-------------------------

948126 -- LITE  SHRIMP  SALAD

1 lb. shrimp, boiled & chopped
1/4 c. onions, chopped
1 c. Kraft's no-fat, no cholesterol
   mayonnaise
3 boiled eggs (use only 1 yolk)
1/4 c. celery, chopped
Dash of garlic powder
Salt & pepper to taste

Mix all ingredients and allow to sit in the refrigerator for 2 hours.

-------------------------

948127 -- SHRIMP  GUMBO

1 ham hock, cut up
5 to 6 tomatoes
1 c. celery, chopped
1 onion, dropped
1 lb. shrimp
1 1/4 c. cut okra
2 c. fresh corn
1 tsp. sugar
2 c. rice, cooked

Measure 4 to 6 cups water in large pot (chicken broth, may be used). Add tomatoes, celery, onions, corn and ham. Bring to boil then reduce heat and simmer for 2 1/2 hours. Last 20 minutes add shrimp, okra and rice.

------------------------

948128 -- SEAFOOD CHOWDER

1/2 lb. scallops
1/3 lb. shrimp
1/4 lb. lobster
1 c. minced clams
1 bottle clam juice
1 can evaporated milk
2 c. cream
1 sm. onion, chopped
2 tsp. butter
1 c. potatoes, bite-sized
1/4 tsp. paprika
1/4 tsp. pepper
Salt to taste

Brown onion in butter. Add clams, clam juice and potatoes. Cook 10 minutes or until potatoes are tender. Add remaining ingredients and simmer for 30 minutes.
Serves 4.

------------------------

948129 -- SHRIMP SALAD

2 (4 1/2 oz.) cans shrimp
1 1/2 c. cooked rice
1 c. celery, chopped
2 tbsp. sweet pickle relish or sweet
    pickle juice
1/2 c. mayonnaise or enough to mix
    well
Salt and pepper to taste

Canned shrimp is usually salty so it is easy to over-salt and lose the shrimp taste. Rice can be added to make a larger quantity, also celery.

------------------------

948130 -- SHRIMP SOUP

1/4 c. chopped green onions
1 clove garlic, minced
1/2 tbsp. cayenne pepper
1 tbsp. margarine
2 cans cream of potato soup
1 (3 oz.) pkg. cream cheese
1 1/2 soup cans of milk
2 c. cleaned shrimp
1 can corn

Cook green onions, garlic in margarine until tender. Add cayenne, soup, cream cheese, milk, shrimp and corn. Bring to boil. Reduce heat. Cover. Simmer 10 minutes. Stir occasionally.

------------------------

## 948131 -- SALMON CHOWDER

5 slices bacon
1 tbsp. bacon drippings
3/4 c. chopped onion
3 tbsp. flour
1/2 tsp. salt
1/4 tsp. pepper
1 (15 oz.) can salmon; remove skin &
   bones, drain, reserve liquid
2 med.-sized raw potatoes, cubed or
2 c. milk

1. In breakfast skillet, fry bacon over medium-low heat until crisp. Drain on paper toweling. Reserve bacon drippings. Crumble bacon. 2. In skillet, combine bacon drippings and onion. Saute over medium-low heat until golden brown, about 5 minutes. 3. Combine flour, salt and pepper. Add to onion mixture, stir. Measure salmon liquid, add water to make 3 cups. Gradually add to onion mixture over medium heat. 4. Transfer onion-liquid mixture to 3-quart saucepan. Add potatoes; bring mixture to a boil over medium heat. Cover, reduce heat to low and simmer for 20 minutes or until potatoes are tender. Stir occasionally. 5. Add salmon, milk and crumbled bacon. Heat over low heat until heated thoroughly, about 8 minutes. Stir occasionally. Makes 6 servings.
NOTE: One or two 16 ounce cans of potatoes can be substituted for the raw potatoes, eliminating approximately 20 minutes of preparation.

------------------------

## 948133 -- SEAFOOD PASTA SALAD

1/2 c. mayonnaise
1/4 c. Italian dressing (preferably
   "Zesty")
1/4 c. Parmesan cheese
8 oz. Ro-tel (corkscrew) pasta,
   cooked & drained
8 oz. imitation crab or lobster meat,
   cut in chunks
1/2 to 1 c. broccoli, partially cooked
1 tomato, chopped

Combine mayonnaise, dressing and cheese; mix well. Add crab meat, broccoli and tomato; mix well. Add pasta, mix. Chill for 15 minutes.

------------------------

948134 -- NEIMAN   MARCUS   SEAFOOD   SALAD

2 c. cooked rice, chilled
1/2 c. crabmeat or chopped lobster
1/2 c. slivered ham
1/2 c. celery, finely chopped
2 hard-cooked eggs, finely chopped
1 tbsp. chives, chopped
1/4 c. parsley, chopped
1 tbsp. olive oil
1 tbsp. red wine vinegar
1/2 c. mayonnaise
Salt & pepper to taste

Combine and lightly toss rice, crabmeat, ham, celery, eggs, chives and parsley. Sprinkle with olive oil and red wine vinegar. Add mayonnaise, salt and pepper and mix all together. Chill several hours before serving. Yield 6 servings.

------------------------

948135 -- SALMON   SALAD

1 can red salmon, drained (& I prefer
   to remove bones & dark skin)
3 hard-boiled eggs, diced
1 1/2 c. diced celery
3/4 c. Miracle Whip to which is added
1/3 c. sugar &
1/2 c. sweet pickle relish with juice

Mix last 3 ingredients thoroughly and add to first 3 ingredients.   Chill and serve cold.

------------------------

948136 -- SHRIMPARONI   SALAD

1/2 pkg. Creamette med. shells,
　　uncooked
1 pkg. (10 oz.) frozen cooked shrimp,
　　thawed and drained
1 1/2 c. chopped celery
1 sm. cucumber quartered and sliced
2/3 c. mayonnaise
1/3 c. sour cream
2 tbsp. horseradish sauce
1 tbsp. grated onion
1 tsp. seasoned salt
1/2 tsp. pepper

Prepare shells according to package directions, drain.   In large bowl, combine shells, shrimp, celery and cucumber.   In small bowl, blend mayonnaise, sour cream, horseradish sauce, onion, seasoned salt and pepper.   Add to shells mixture; toss to coat.   Cover:   chill thoroughly.   Toss gently before serving.
Garnish as desired.   Serves 4 to 6 servings.

------------------------

948137 -- MACARONI   SALMON   SALAD

2 c. cooked and cooled macaroni, 1 c.
　　broken, uncooked
1 c. diced cucumber
8 oz. can salmon, flaked
3/4 c. mayonnaise
1/4 tsp. pepper
1 tbsp. grated onion
1 tbsp. minced parsley
1/2 tsp. salt

Combine all ingredients; toss together until blended.   Serve hot or cold.
Serves 4 to 6.

------------------------

948138 -- SOLANA   BEACH   SEAFOOD   PASTA   SALAD

2 tsp. salt, optional
2 tsp. oil, optional
2 lbs. multi colored rotelle pasta, cooked and drained
2 cans (3 3/4 oz. each) Bumble Bee smoked oysters
2 cans ( 7 1/2 oz. each) Bumble Bee red or pink salmon
1 can (12 1/2 oz.) Bumble Bee solid or chunk white tuna
1 can (8 oz.) Bumble Bee whole oysters, drained
1 each small red and green pepper, julienned
1/2 cucumber peeled, quartered and sliced 1/4 inch thick
1/4 c. sliced ripe olives
1/4 c. minced parsley
1/4 c. capers, optional
1/2 c. light cream cheese
1 c. low calorie vinaigrette dressing
Green leaf lettuce
Lemon wedges

Prepare and measure all ingredients. Whisk softened cheese with vinigiarette. Fold ingredients into mixture and chill. Layer serving dish with lettuce leaves and spoon salad mixture on top. Garnish with lemon wedges.

------------------------

## 948139 -- OYSTER BISQUE

1 pt. oysters, chopped & juice
1 onion
1 stalk celery
Parsley
Thyme
1 tbsp. butter
1 tbsp flour
1 pint cream
Salt
Pepper
Nutmeg

Put oysters in a saucepan, add enough water to the oyster juice to make 1 cup.

Add 1 slice onion and a bouquet of celery leaves, parsley, and thyme. Simmer 10 minutes. Remove herbs and puree oysters and onions and add to a sauce made of butter, flour and the pint of cream. Season with salt, pepper and a little nutmeg.

------------------------

## 948140 -- BAKED SEAFOOD BISQUE

1/2 c. butter
1 1/2 c. flour
1 qt. milk
1 tsp. salt
1/2 tsp. pepper
3 c. grated cheese
1/2 c. bread crumbs
1/4 c. cooking sherry
18 to 24 oz. frozen seafood

Make white sauce from butter, flour, milk and seasonings. When thickened, add cheese and sherry. Combine with thawed seafood. At this point, it may be refrigerated or frozen. Put in individual oven proof dishes. Top with remaining cheese and crumbs. Bake at 425 degrees for 10 to 20 minutes until brown and bubbly. Serves 4 to 6.

------------------------

## 948141 -- SHRIMP ROUMALADE

1/3 c. salad oil
1 tsp. salt
1/2 tsp. pepper
1 tsp. real horseradish
2 tbsp. vinegar
4 tsp. hot mustard
1 c. fine chopped celery
1 tsp. fresh parsley
1/4 c. fine chopped green onions
Shrimp, clean, cooked, cold
Hard-cooked eggs
Cherry tomatoes

Can be made 3 to 4 days in advance. Mix in jar and cool. Put clean, cooked shrimp on bed of lettuce. Sprinkle chopped hard-cooked eggs over shrimp, pour roumalade over everything. Cherry tomato on the side.

------------------------

### 948142 -- SHRIMP SALAD

3 c. cooked rice
1 sm. jar hot cauliflower with
    pimento, chopped
1 sm. jar stuffed olives, sliced
3/4 lb. small deveined shrimp or 2 (6
    oz.) cans of shrimp
2 tbsp. lemon juice

About 3/4 cup best foods mayonnaise, salt and pepper to taste. Add chopped onions. Chill well.

------------------------

### 948143 -- CRAB OR SHRIMP LOUIS SALAD

--SALAD:--

Torn salad greens
2 c. crab or shrimp meat
Tomato wedges
Egg wedges
Canned asparagus
Avocado slices

--LOUIS DRESSING:--

1/2 c. refrigerated style French
    dressing
1/3 c. bottled chile sauce or catsup
2 tbsp. mayonnaise
1/2 tsp. Worcestershire sauce
1 tbsp. lemon juice
1/4 black pepper

Prepare and chill dressing by mixing all the ingredients. On serving plate arrange salad greens, mount seafood in center and garnish with vegetables. Serve with Louis dressing. Information Services

------------------------

### 948144 -- CRABMEAT SALAD

1 lb. imitation crabmeat, chopped
1/2 c. chopped celery
1/2 c. chopped green pepper
2 tbsp. minced onion
2 to 3 tbsp. pickle relish
1 c. mayonnaise
2 to 3 tbsp. Hidden Valley Ranch
   dressing
1/2 tsp. Mrs. Dash Seasoning
1 tsp. powdered lemonade mix (or 1/2
   tsp. juice)

Mix all ingredients in large bowl. Chill and serve. Serve with crackers as a side dish. VARIATIONS: Add any of the following: A. (thawed) frozen peas about 1/2 cup. B. shredded Colby or cheddar cheese. C. cooked pasta (3 to 4 cups). D. Use your imagination.

------------------------

## 948145 -- SHRIMP MACARONI SALAD

1 qt. mayonnaise
1/4 c. olive oil
2 tbsp. Worcestershire sauce
2 tbsp. lemon juice
1 1/2 tbsp. poupon mustard
3 tsp. salt
2 tbsp. hot sauce
2 lbs. macaroni, cooked
2 doz. eggs, chopped
2 c. onion, chopped
2 c. dill pickles, chopped
2 c. celery, chopped
Black olives
2 lbs. cooked salad shrimp

Mix all dressing ingredients together, add rest of ingredients; mix well.

------------------------

## 948146 -- CREAM OF CRAB SOUP

1 lb. Maryland Backfin Crabmeat
1/4 c. (1/2 stick) butter or margarine
1/3 c. flour
1 c. chicken broth

1/4 tsp. pepper
5 c. milk
Salt to taste

Remove cartilage from crabmeat, melt butter in 3-quart pan. Blend in flour and stir until smooth. Slowly stir in chicken broth and pepper. Simmer for 2 minutes. Add milk and cook slowly, stirring constantly until thickened. Do not boil. Add crabmeat to milk mixture and salt to taste. Remove from heat and serve. Makes about 10 cups.

------------------------

948147 -- SHRIMP   SALAD

1 box ring macaroni, cooked
3 hard-boiled eggs, diced
20 stuffed olives, diced
1 celery stalk, chopped fine
1 green onion, chopped fine
Frozen tiny salad shrimp, cooked

--DRESSING:--

1/3 c. French or Western dressing
1/3 c. mayonnaise
1/4 c. whipped cream
Salt & pepper to taste

Mix all ingredients, toss with dressing, refrigerate. May substitute ham, tuna or chicken (diced) for shrimp. Electronics

------------------------

948148 -- CRAB   &   PEA   SALAD

1 (6 1/2 oz.) can crab meat
1 c. cooked peas
1 c. cooked white rice
1/4 tsp. curry powder
1/4 c. mayonnaise
1/4 tsp. paprika

Mix together, cover and refrigerate at least 1 hour before serving.

------------------------

### 948149 -- SPINACH CRAB SOUP

1 (7 oz.) can crabmeat
10 oz. pkg. chopped spinach
3 tbsp. butter
1 c. diced celery
1/2 c. onion
2 tbsp. flour
1/2 tsp. salt
1/8 tsp. pepper
1/8 tsp. nutmeg
2 c. chicken broth, College Inn
2 c. half and half

Drain crabmeat, save liquid. Cook spinach. Melt butter in large saucepan. Add celery and onions and saute until tender. Blend in flour, salt, pepper and nutmeg. Gradually add broth, stirring constantly. Heat to a boil. Add half and half and crab liquid. Stir in crab and spinach. Cook for at least 1/2 hour.

------------------------

### 948150 -- WILD RICE & SHRIMP SALAD

1 c. wild rice or 1 pkg. long grain &
   wild rice
1 c. chili sauce
2 tbsp. prepared horseradish
1 tbsp. lemon juice
1 lb. shrimp, peeled, deveined,
   cooked & cut in half lengthwise
2 tbsp. chopped parsley

Cook rice. Transfer to a large bowl. Meanwhile, combine chili sauce, horseradish and lemon juice in small bowl. Add shrimp and chili sauce mixture to rice, tossing to mix well. Cover and chill until ready to serve. Fold in parsley and spoon onto beds of lettuce.

------------------------

### 948152 -- CRAB SALAD

16 oz. crab meat
2/3 c. mayonnaise

2/3 c. celery, finely sliced
2 tsp. lemon juice

Mix mayonnaise and lemon juice in 2 quart bowl. Add celery and shrimp. Refrigerate until served.

------------------------

## 948153 -- MEAT OR SEAFOOD PASTA SALAD

Combine dressing and cheese, mix well: 1/2 c. Miracle Whip
1/4 c. Zesty Italian dressing
2 tbsp. grated Parmesan cheese

2 c. cooked corkscrew noodles
1 1/2 c. seafood or meat
1 c. broccoli flowerets
1/2 c. green pepper, chopped
1/2 c. tomatoes, chopped
1/4 c. green onions

------------------------

## 948154 -- SHRIMP SALAD

1 pkg. Uncle Bens long grain (wild rice), prepare, cool
6 hard-boiled eggs, diced
2 lbs. cooked shrimp
1 1/2 c. diced celery
1 c. salad dressing
1/4 tsp. garlic powder
1/4 c. diced onion
1/4 tsp. celery salt

Mix together and chill.

------------------------

## 948155 -- CRABMEAT PASTA SALAD

2 lbs. imitation crabmeat, chopped
3 1/2 c. macaroni shells
1 green pepper, chopped
4 stalks celery, chopped

1/2 c. grated onion
1 tsp. sugar
1/2 tsp. vinegar
1/4 tsp. curry powder
Salt & pepper to taste
3/4 c. mayonnaise
4 hard-boiled eggs, chopped
1/2 tsp. paprika
1/2 tsp. parsley

  Boil macaroni and drain and cool.   Combine with all remaining ingredients.   Chill for at least 2 hours.   Serve.

------------------------

948156 -- SEAFOOD   SALAD

1 lb. Chilean shrimp
1 lb. Chilean langostinos
1 lb. sea scallops, cooked
8 sea legs, sliced
3 green peppers
1 med. onion
1/2 c. celery
8 oz. Italian salad dressing

  Combine all the above.   Pour Italian salad dressing in salad and toss.   Chill.   Serves 8 to 10.

------------------------

948157 -- SHRIMP   SALAD

1 pkg. lemon Jello
1 c. chili sauce
1 tbsp. lemon juice
Celery, if desired
1 c. hot water
1 or 2 tbsp. horseradish
1 c. small shrimp

  Mix together and pour into mold, chill and serve.

------------------------

948158 -- SHRIMP   GUMBO

1 c. celery, chopped
1 c. green peppers, chopped
1 c. onions, chopped, may use green
   onions

In a large kettle, cover with water and cook until tender, about 10 - 15 minutes.

--ADD AND BRING TO BOIL:--

1 can okra, wash if desired
1 can stewed tomatoes
1 lg. can tomato juice or vegetable
   juice

Salt and pepper to taste
1 tsp. cumin
1 tsp. gumbo file

Add one pound shrimp or 2 cans of shrimp. Bring back to boil. Serve over steamed rice in soup bowls. Serve with crackers or rolls, salad and a light dessert. Add leftover rice to leftover soup and store in containers in the freezer. Makes a quick lunch. I joined the Auxiliary in 1964 at my husbands urging, but wasn't regular in attendance for several years as there were children in school, Church, 4 P.T.A's, Cub Scouts, and Girl Scouts. There are always things that need doing no matter what group you belong to.

------------------------

948159 -- DICED  SHRIMP  SALAD

1 pkg. dried shrimp
3 bunches leaf onion
4 tomatoes

Soak shrimp in water for 1 - 2 hours. Dice up onions. Dice tomatoes into small pieces. Drain the shrimp, leaving a little bit of water. Put the onions and tomatoes in with the shrimp and mix well. Season to taste. Serve on a lettuce cup.

------------------------

948160 -- CRAB  SALAD

2 (3 oz.) pkg. lemon Jello
4 c. tomato juice
2 cans crab, drained and flaked

3 c. celery, chopped
3 tbsp. onion, grated
1 1/2 tbsp. Worcestershire sauce
1 1/2 tbsp. vinegar

Dissolve Jello in 1 cup hot juice. Add remaining 3 cups tomato juice. Add the remainder of the ingredients. Refrigerate until firm.

------------------------

### 948161 -- SHRIMP-CRABMEAT SALAD

1 lg. loaf sandwich bread
4 eggs, hard boiled and chopped
1 lg. onion, chopped fine
1/4 c. pimiento, chopped
3 c. mayonnaise
1 1/2 c. celery, chopped
2 cans shrimp, drained
1 can crabmeat, drained
3 tbsp. Shedd's sauce (optional)

Remove crusts from the bread. Butter both sides and then cube. Add the eggs and onion. Refrigerate overnight. Add the shrimp, crabmeat, celery, pimiento, mayonnaise and Shedd's. Mix well and refrigerate 3 - 4 hours before serving.

------------------------

### 948162 -- SHRIMP SALAD

1 pkg. ring macaroni, cooked
1 or 2 grated carrots
1 med. onion, diced
1 c. celery
1 can shrimp, drained or 1 pkg.
    frozen shrimp
1/2 bag frozen peas, cooked & cooled

--DRESSING:--

1 1/2 c. salad dressing
1/3 c. sugar
1/4 c. lemon juice
1 tsp. salt
Dash of pepper

Combine first 6 ingredients. Mix dressing and pour over all. This is better if made a day ahead and allowed to flavor through. May add pimento olives, radishes, green pepper. Three cups of chicken or turkey. May be used in place of shrimp. Pam Vogel

------------------------

948163 -- CRAB-ROTINI SALAD

2 lbs. rotini pasta, boiled, drained & cooled
1 lb. imitation crab meat, shredded
1/2 cucumber, diced
3-4 radish, sliced
4 scallions, sliced
Fresh broccoli flowerettes (optional)
3 ribs celery, diced
1/4 c. fresh parsley (remove stems & chop fine)
1 red pepper, diced

--DRESSING:--

1/2 (6 oz.) bottle Thousand Island dressing
1 (12 oz.) bottle Italian dressing
Salt & pepper to taste
Paprika & sugar to taste

------------------------

948164 -- RICE AND SHRIMP SALAD

3 c. cold cooked rice
1 c. boiled shrimp
6 hard-cooked eggs, sliced
1 c. sweet or sour pickles, diced
Salt and pepper to taste
1 c. celery, diced
1 c. stuffed olives, finely chopped
Salad dressing

Combine all ingredients. Garnish with additional hard-cooked eggs. Yield: 6-8 servings.

------------------------

## 948165 -- SEAFOOD SALAD

--DRESSING:--

1/2 c. mayonnaise
1/4 c. sour cream
2 tsp. lemon juice
2 tsp. dill weed
1/8 tsp. pepper

Combine all ingredients; blend throughly. --SALAD:--

1 (8 oz.) pkg. sealegs (crab-flavored
    white fish)
1/4 c. chopped green onion
1/4 c. chopped celery
2 hard-cooked eggs, chopped

Combine sealegs, onion, celery and eggs. Add dressing and toss lightly to mix. May also be used as sandwich filling or with crackers for appetizer. Yields: 4 servings.

------------------------

## 948166 -- SALMON RICE SALAD

2 c. cooked, cooled rice
1 c. celery, sliced
1/2 c. green onions, sliced
1/2 c. sweet pickle relish
1 c. salad dressing or mayonnaise (I
    use mayonnaise)
1/2 tsp. black pepper
2 cans Chicken of the Sea boneless
    pink salmon
1/2 c. red pepper, chopped
1/2 c. sliced almonds or Pine Nuts (I
    use almonds)
1 c. frozen peas, thawed (I don't use
    peas)

Combine all ingredients and toss lightly. Chill. Serve on lettuce leaves. Serves 6.

------------------------

## 948167 -- CRAB AND SPINACH CHOWDER

6-8 oz. crab meat, thawed or canned
1 (10 oz.) pkg. frozen whole spinach
3 tbsp. butter
1/2 c. chopped onion
2 tbsp. flour
1/2 tsp. salt
1 pinch white pepper
1 pinch ground nutmeg
2 c. chicken broth
2 c. dairy cream, med.

Cut crab into bite-size pieces (reserve liquid). Cook spinach slightly, drain and chop coarsely. Melt butter in large pot. Add onion and saute until tender. Blend in flour and seasonings. Gradually add chicken broth, stirring constantly. Heat to boiling. Add cream and reserved crab liquid. Stir in crab meat and spinach. Cook until heated through. Makes 4 to 6 servings. VFA 125 FRAMP Admin

------------------------

948168 -- SEAFOOD  (CIOPINNO)  CHOWDER

Sm. onion, chopped
Clove garlic, minced
Stalk of celery, chopped
1 sm. carrot, chopped
Oil to saute
1/4 tsp. each of basil & oregano
2 c. chicken stock or bouillon
1 c. water or clam broth
1/2 lb. shrimp, 1/2 lb. scallops or
    your favorite white fish, cut up
Cooked rice
Salt & pepper to taste

Saute chopped vegetables lightly in oil. Add 2 cups chicken broth plus water or clam broth and seasonings. Simmer 15 minutes. Then add seafood, cook 10 minutes longer. For variation: You may add 1 can stewed tomatoes when adding the broth. Serve with cooked rice.

------------------------

948169 -- SEAFOOD  CHOWDER

1 tbsp. vegetable oil
1 c. minced onion

1 clove garlic, minced
1/4 tsp. dried dillweed, crushed
1 can (10 3/4 oz.) Campbell's
   condensed cream of celery soup
1 can (10 3/4 oz.) Campbell's
   condensed cream of potato soup
1 1/2 soup cans of milk
1/2 lb. med. shrimp, shelled &
   deveined
1/2 lb. firm whitefish fillets, cut
   into 2 inch pieces
Chopped fresh parsley for garnish

1. In 3 quart saucepan, over medium heat, cook onion, garlic and dill in hot oil, stirring occasionally until onion is tender. 2. Stir in soups and milk. Heat to boiling, stirring often. Cook 8 minutes. Reduce heat to low. 3. Add shrimp and fish. Cook 5 minutes more or until shrimp turn pink and opaque and fish flakes easily when tested with fork, stirring occasionally. 4. To serve, ladle soup into bowls. Garnish with parsley. Serves 4.

------------------------

948170 -- SEAFOOD   SALAD

1 lb. med. shrimp
1 lb. crab meat
3 stalks celery
1 lg. onion
1 tbsp. garlic powder
1 1/2 tsp. lemon pepper powder
1 tsp. paprika
1/4 c. mayonnaise
1/2 c. sour cream

Mix and chill before serving.

------------------------

948171 -- RUTH'S   MACARONI   &   SHRIMP

1 c. shrimp (1 can cut in halves)
1 sm. can pimientos
1 green pepper
4 hard-boiled eggs
1 sm. onion (green onions)
Salt to taste

Add 1 1/2 cups uncooked macaroni to salted water (boiling). Cook until tender, drain, rinse with cold water. Mix with salad dressing turned with cream.

------------------------

948172 -- CRAB BISQUE THIRTY SEVENTH

From Elizabeth on 37th , one of Savannah's most popular restaurants. 6 tbsp. butter
1 c. green onion, minced
1/2 c. celery, minced
1 tbsp. carrots, minced
6 tbsp. flour
2 1/2 c. milk
2 1/2 c. chicken broth
1/4 tsp. nutmeg
1/4 tsp. white pepper
1 c. cream
1/4 c. good sherry
1 lb. claw crab meat, picked over

Melt butter over low heat in saucepan. Add minced onion, celery and carrot and cover, sweat until tender, about 5 minutes. Whisk in flour and cook 2 minutes. Whisk in milk and broth. Bring to a boil, whisking occasionally. Add seasonings, cream, sherry and crab. Serve immediately. Serves 12. (This is easy and delicious.)

------------------------

948173 -- SPICY CRAB SOUP

1 qt. water
6 chicken wings
3 lbs. canned tomatoes, quartered
1 (8 oz.) frozen corn, thawed
1 c. frozen peas, thawed
3/4 c. celery, chopped
3/4 c. onion, diced
3/4 tbsp. seafood seasoning
1 tsp. salt
1/4 tsp. lemon pepper
1 lb. Maryland crabmeat, fresh or
    pasteurized, (regular or claw)

Place water and chicken in a large pan. Cover and simmer over low heat for at least one hour. Add vegetables and seasonings and simmer, covered, over medium heat about 30 to 40 minutes or until vegetables are almost done. Add crabmeat, cover and simmer 15 minutes more.  Serve hot.  (If a milder soup is desired, decrease seafood seasoning.)   Yield:   8 servings at 153 calories per serving.

------------------------

948174 -- SEAFOOD   CHOWDER

1 chopped onion
1 stick celery, chopped

1 c. water (or more)
2 cubed potatoes

Cook 10 to 15 minutes.  Add enough flour to thicken.  Add: 1 to 1 1/2 cubes of chicken bouillon
1 can clams
1 can shrimp (or fresh)
1 c. milk
1 c. light cream
1 slice American cheese (optional)
Pinch of white pepper
1 bay leaf
Pinch of thyme
Few drops Worcestershire sauce

Cook a few minutes until cooked.

------------------------

948175 -- SHRIMP   SOUP

2 cans Campbells cream of potato soup
2 can creamed corn
1 (8 oz.) pkg. cream cheese
1 pkg. salad shrimp
2 soup cans of milk

Heat all ingredients together until cream cheese is melted.

------------------------

948176 -- SEAFOOD   PASTA   SALAD

1/2 c. Miracle Whip
1/4 c. Kraft Zesty Italian dressing
2 tbsp. Kraft Parmesan cheese

2 c. corkscrew noodles, cooked,
   drained & cooled
1 1/2 c. chopped imitation crabmeat
1 c. broccoli flowerets, partially
   cooked
1/2 c. green peppers
1/2 c. chopped tomatoes
1/4 c. green onion slices

Combine dressings and cheese. Mix well. Add remaining ingredients. Mix lightly. Chill well.

------------------------

948177 -- SHRIMP  BISQUE

1/4 c. each finely chopped onion,
   celery
2 tbsp. flour
1 tsp. butter flavored salt
1/4 tsp. paprika
Dash of white pepper
4 c. skim milk
14 oz. cooked shrimp, coarsely chopped

Combine first 2 ingredients with 1/4 cup water in saucepan. Simmer until veggies are tender. Add remaining ingredients except shrimp, mixing well. Simmer until thick, stirring constantly. Fold in shrimp, heat to serving temperature. Yields: 6.

------------------------

948178 -- SHRIMP  &  BEER  BISQUE

1 (12 oz.) bottle of beer
3 to 4 peppercorns
1 bay leaf
1 lb. shelled, deveined shrimp
1 qt. light cream
Salt & white pepper
Fresh parsley for garnish

Put the beer in a saucepan with the peppercorns and bay leaf. Bring just to a boil and add the shrimp. When the shrimp are pink, and before they curl up tight, they are done. Remove saucepan from the heat. Strain the beer into a container and refrigerate it. Rinse the shrimp under cold water to stop the cooking and refrigerate separately. Puree the shrimp, with the cool beer stock, saving enough whole shrimp for garnish.  Stir in the cream and season with salt  and white pepper.  Chill thoroughly.  Serve in chilled bowls, with fresh parsley and the reserved shrimp. Serves 4 to 6.

------------------------

948179 -- SHRIMP   SALAD

1 lb. baby Maine shrimp
1/2 sm. onion
1 stalk of celery
2 tbsp. fresh parsley, chopped
2 tsp. lemon juice
1/2 tsp. salt
1/4 tsp. white pepper
Mayonnaise to taste

Mince the onion and celery, chop the parsley and mix it all together.   3 to 4   servings.

------------------------

948180 -- CRAB   JELLO   SALAD

1 sm. pkg. lemon Jello
1 sm. pkg. lime Jello
1 c. chopped celery
1 can crabmeat, drained & flaked
4 hard-boiled eggs, chopped
1 c. salad dressing
Additional dressing

Prepare Jello according to package directions.  Chill until thickened.  Fold celery, crabmeat, egg and salad dressing into congealed mixture.  Chill until set.  Serve dressing in a separate dish.

------------------------

948181 -- SHRIMP   RICE   CAULIFLOWER   SALAD

2 bags boil in a bag rice, success
   rice cooked
1 cauliflower coarsley chopped
2 green peppers coarsely chopped
6 stalks celery coarsely chopped
1 1/2 to 2 lb. shrimp, steamed and
   shelled

1 pkg. imitation crab meat drained
   and chopped
1 tsp. salt

Toss all together in large bowl. Bind with salad dressing. I use a combination Marzettis slaw dressing and Miracle Whip.

------------------------

948182 -- SHRIMP SALAD

1/2 lb. sm. shelled salad shrimp
3/4 lb. shell noodles, cooked
1 tsp. salt to taste
1/2 c. chopped celery
1/2 c. chopped green onion
1 reg. can peas
1 c. or more of Best Food mayonnaise
   to moisten

Mix together. Store in refrigerator until time to serve.

------------------------

948183 -- ZESTY CRAB LOUIE SALAD

2 pkgs. (3 oz. each) Ramen Pride
   Shrimp flavor
4 c. water
1/4 c. seasoned rice vinegar
1/2 c. mayonnaise
1/4 c. sliced green onion
1/4 c. ketchup
8 oz. cooked crab meat
1/2 c. sliced celery
1/2 c. sliced ripe olives

1. Before opening packages, break noodles and remove flavor packets. 2. In 2 quart pan bring water to a boil and add contents of one flavor packet and noodles. Cook for 3 minutes. Drain, rinse and chill. 3. Combine contents of remaining flavor packet, vinegar, mayonnaise, and ketchup. Mix well. 4. In large bowl combine crabmeat, celery, olives, and green onion. Mix with dressing. Toss with chilled noodles.

------------------------

948184 -- CRAB PASTA SALAD

4 oz. uncooked pasta
8 oz. chopped crab meat
1/2 c. celery, chopped
1/2 c. onion, chopped
1/4 c. green pepper, chopped
2 tbsp. parsley
1/2 c. mayonnaise
1/2 c. sour cream
1/4 c. chili sauce
2 tbsp. Dijon mustard

Cook pasta and drain. Combine pasta, crab meat, celery, onion, green pepper and parsley. Add remaining ingredients. Mix well. Chill and serve.

------------------------

## 948185 -- A DIETER'S DREAM SHRIMP SALAD

6 oz. frozen sm. shrimp
1 (16 oz.) can cut green beans
1 garlic clove
1 tbsp. salad oil
1/4 tsp. dry mustard
1/2 tsp. sugar
1/4 c. vinegar
2 chicken bouillon cubes
2/3 c. rice, cooked
1 c. celery, sliced
1/2 c. sweet onion, sliced
2 c. lettuce, shredded
Soy sauce (optional)

Rinse frozen shrimp. Chill can of green beans. Drain and save liquid. Slice thinly the garlic clove and crush in large bowl. Add oil, mustard, sugar, vinegar, shrimp and beans. Refrigerate. Heat bean liquid. Add bouillon cubes and stir until dissolved. Add enough water to make 2 cups. Add rice. Bring to a boil and cook rapidly, uncovered, about 8 minutes or until rice stands above the water line. Reduce heat to lowest point, cover and steam for 12 to 14 minutes. Spread rice in a shallow pan to cool. Refrigerate for 10 minutes or until needed at serving time. Add rice to shrimp and bean mixture. Toss together with celery, onion and lettuce. Serve with soy sauce.

------------------------

## 948186 -- SHRIMP SALAD

1 to 2 lbs. med. shrimp, boil, shell & devein
2 c. broccoli florets
Green onions to taste (8, more or less), cut in pieces
1 or 2 (8 oz.) cans artichoke hearts, drained (water packed)
Salt & fresh ground pepper to taste
1 c. sherry mayonnaise (1/4 c. dry sherry added to Hellmann's is fine)

Drop shrimp in boiling salted water for 3 minutes. Drain in colander and cool with ice cubes. Shell and devein. Steam florets 3 to 5 minutes. Do not overcook. Cool in ice water to retain bright green color. Drain well and set aside. Quarter or halve drained artichokes and combine in bowl with shrimp, broccoli and scallions. Add salt and pepper, sherry, mayonnaise and toss. Cover and refrigerate. This recipe easy to adjust for the number you want to serve. 4 to 8 servings.

------------------------

948187 -- SHE-CRAB SOUP

"She-crab" is much more of a delicacy than "he-crab", as the eggs add a special flavor to the soup. The Street vendors make a point of calling "shecrab" loudly and of charging extra for them. 1 tbsp. butter
1 qt. milk
1/4 pt. cream, whipped
Few drops onion juice
1/8 tsp. mace
1/8 tsp. pepper
1/2 tsp. Worcestershire sauce
1 tsp. flour
2 c. white crab meat & crab eggs
1/2 tsp. salt
4 tbsp. dry sherry

Melt butter in top of double boiler and blend with flour until smooth. Add the milk gradually, stirring constantly. To this add crab meat and eggs and all seasonings except sherry. Cook slowly over hot water for 20 minutes. To serve, place 1 tablespoon of warmed sherry in individual soup bowls, then add soup and top with whipped cream. Sprinkle paprika or finely chopped parsley on top.
Secret: If unable to obtain "she-crabs", crumble yolk of hard-boiled eggs in bottom of soup plates. Serves 4 to 6.

------------------------

## 948188 -- SEAFOOD CHOWDER

1 lg. onion, chopped
2 lbs. imitation crab meat, shrimp and/or scallops, chopped
1/2 stick butter
1 qt. cubed potatoes
3 c. light cream
Salt, pepper, nutmeg & paprika to taste
1 sm. can chicken broth
Flour

Saute chopped seafood with onions in butter 10 minutes. Add cream, broth and spices. Thicken as needed with flour to a creamy consistency. Add potatoes. Cook 20 minutes (low simmer).

------------------------

## 948189 -- ITALIAN RAVIOLI AND SEAFOOD SOUP

Seafood alternatives: Scallops, rockfish, grouper

Italian stewed tomatoes provide all the seasoning needed for this light, but filling, soup. We suggest a variety of seafood, but you can increase the amount of just one if you like.

1 (8 to 10 oz.) pkg. fresh or frozen cheese ravioli
1 (28 oz.) can Italian stewed tomatoes
2 (14 1/2 oz.) cans chicken broth
18 med. shrimp, shelled & deveined
1 lb. halibut steak, cut into 1/2" wide strips
1 sm. can (1 1/2 oz.) Parmesan cheese

Cook ravioli according to package directions. Pour into a colander, rinse in cold water until cooled and set aside. To a 4 to 5 quart pan, add tomatoes and their liquid and chicken broth; cover and bring to a boil. Add pasta to pan then drop shrimp and fish strips on top. Cover and simmer until fish is opaque in center, 4 to 6 minutes. Divide seafood among 6 bowls then add ravioli and soup. Sprinkle each serving with Parmesan cheese. Makes 6 servings. Per serving: 290 cal.; 40 g prot.; 14 g carbo.; 1.8 g sat.; 1.6 g mono.; 1 g poly.; .8 g om-3; 167 mg chol.; 646 mg sod.

------------------------

## 948190 -- ANDES SHRIMP & CORN MAIN-DISH CHOWDER

1/4 c. chopped green onions
1 sm. clove garlic, minced
1/8 tbsp. cayenne pepper
2 cans cream of potato soup
1 (3 oz.) pkg. cream cheese, softened
1 1/2 soup cans milk
2 c. frozen, cleaned raw shrimp
1 (8 oz.) can whole kernel corn, not
   drained

In saucepan, cook onions with garlic, cayenne pepper, and butter until tender. Blend soup, cream cheese and milk. Add shrimp and corn. Bring to boil, stirring often. Reduce heat and cover. Simmer 10 minutes or until done.

------------------------

## 948191 -- SHRIMP - RICE - CAULIFLOWER SALAD

2 bags, boil in a bag, rice cooked
1 head cauliflower, coarsely chopped
2 green peppers, chopped
8 stalks celery, chopped
2 lbs. shrimp, cooked & shelled
1 pkg. imitation crab meat, drained
1 tsp. salt

Toss together in large bowl. Bind with salad dressing. I use a combination of Marzetti's slaw dressing and Miracle Whip.

------------------------

## 948192 -- SEAFOOD PASTA SALAD

1/2 c. mayonnaise
1/4 c. Italian dressing
1/4 c. grated Parmesan cheese
2 c. (8 oz.) corkscrew noodles,
   cooked & drained
8 oz. imitation flowerettes,
   partially cooked
1/2 c. green pepper, chopped
1/2 c. tomato, chopped
1/4 c. green onion slices

Combine dressings and cheese; mix well. Add remaining ingredients; mix lightly. Chill. Serve with freshly ground black pepper if desired.

------------------------

### 948193 -- SEAFOOD BISQUE

1 can cream of chicken soup
1 can cream of mushroom soup
1 can cream of celery soup
2 c. half & half

Heat together. 3 c. shrimp, lobster and/or crab
3/4 c. sherry or white wine

Garnish with cheese, or croutons, or almonds, or parsley. Serves 4 to 6.

------------------------

### 948194 -- CURRIED SHRIMP SOUP

1/4 c. butter
3 tbsp. flour (instant blending)
1 qt. milk
9 oz. shrimp, cut
2 tbsp. parsley, minced
1/2 tsp. onion salt
1/2 tsp. curry powder
1/4 tsp. salt

Combine all ingredients in large saucepan. Cook over medium heat, stirring constantly until thickened and hot. Serves 6.

------------------------

### 948195 -- SHRIMP GUMBO

2 tbsp. butter or margarine
1/2 c. bell pepper, chopped
1 clove garlic
1 lg. can whole tomatoes
1 can tomato sauce
1/8 tsp. chili powder
1 tsp. parsley, chopped
1 med. bag of shrimp
1 lg. onion, chopped

2 stalks celery, chopped
1/2 lb. okra, washed & sliced
1 c. water
1 tsp. salt
1/8 tsp. cayenne pepper
1/8 tsp. thyme
1 bay leaf, crushed
1 can crabmeat

Heat butter in a large skillet. Add chopped onion and chopped bell pepper. Add chopped celery and garlic. Cook all until onion is soft. Add okra and can of tomatoes and water, tomato sauce, salt, pepper, cayenne pepper, chili powder, thyme, chopped parsley and bay leaf. Let all simmer until okra is done (1 hour). Taste (may need more garlic and salt.) Add shrimp and crab meat. Let simmer at least 1 hour. Serve over cooked rice.

------------------------

948196 -- CRAB   OR   SHRIMP   GUMBO

1/2 lb. crabmeat or shrimp
1/2 c. celery, chopped
1 clove garlic, chopped
2 1/2 cans whole tomatoes
1/2 tsp. crushed thyme
1/4 tsp. sugar
1/4 lb. butter
1/2 c. onion, chopped
10 oz. okra, diced
2 tsp. salt
Black pepper to taste
1 bay leaf

Cook crabmeat or shrimp until tender in butter after adding celery, onion and garlic. Add okra, tomatoes and seasoning. Simmer, covered, 45 minutes. Remove bay leaf and serve. Good with cooked rice.

------------------------

948197 -- SHRIMP   SALAD

Heat 1 can tomato soup and add 1 (8 ounce) package cream cheese. Blend 2 cups mashed or chopped shrimp. Add: 1 c. celery, finely chopped
1 c. onions, finely chopped
1 c. mayonnaise

1 tsp. (or less) dill weed
1 1/2 pkgs. gelatin

Pour in oiled mold.   Set overnight.

------------------------

## 948198 -- SEAFOOD   SALAD

3 c. shell macaroni, cooked
2 tsp. prepared mustard
2 tbsp. onions (or more)
1/2 c. green pepper, chopped
2 c. boiled shrimp, cut up
1/2 c. salad dressing
1 c. celery
2 tbsp. pickle relish
1 can tuna fish
Garlic salt (sprinkle on top)

Mix all together and refrigerate, covered, until serving time.

------------------------

## 948199 -- GOURMET   CRAB   RING

1 tsp. unflavored gelatin
1/4 c. cold water
2 (8 oz.) pkgs. cream cheese, softened
2 tbsp. cooking sherry (optional)
1 (2 oz.) jar pimentos, chopped &
   drained
1 (6 oz.) pkg. frozen crabmeat,
   thawed, drained & cut up
3/4 tsp. seasoned salt
1/8 tsp. black pepper
1/4 c. snipped parsley

Sprinkle gelatin over water to soften.  Stir over hot water until dissolved.  Beat into cream cheese until smooth.  Stir in next 5 ingredients and 2 tablespoons parsley. Pour into a mold.  Refrigerate at least 4 hours, or until  set.  To serve, turn out on plate.  Garnish with remaining parsley.  Makes 3 cups spread.

------------------------

## 948200 -- CRABMEAT   SOUP

1 (11 1/4 oz.) can green pea soup
1 (10 1/2 oz.) can tomato soup
2 soup cans milk
1/2 c. light cream
1/4 c. sherry
1 (6 1/2 oz.) can crabmeat, drained &
    cartilage removed

Combine soups in saucepan. Gradually stir in milk. Add cream, sherry and crabmeat. Heat slowly, stirring occasionally. Do not boil. 6 servings.

------------------------

## 948201 -- SEAFOOD PASTA SALAD

1 lb. shrimp
1 lb. crab or imitation crab meat
1 lg. Spanish onion, chopped
10 oz. salad size shell pasta, cooked
    & drained
1/2 green pepper, chopped
1/2 red pepper, chopped (optional)

Mix together in large bowl. --DRESSING:--

1/2 c. mayonnaise
1 lg. bottle Zesty Italian dressing

Mix ingredients for dressing together. Use Italian dressing to taste. Mix dressing and salad ingredients together. Chill 4 hours or overnight. August 8, 1991

------------------------

## 948202 -- SHRIMP SALAD

1 c. cooked shrimp
3 c. cooked rice
1/2 c. chopped celery
1/4 c. chopped olives
1/4 c. chopped green pepper
1/4 c. minced onion
1 lemon (cut into wedges)
3 tbsp. mayonnaise
2 tomatoes (cut into wedges)
1/4 tsp. pepper

1/2 tsp. salt
Crisp greens to line bowl

Combine shrimp, rice, celery, olives, green pepper, onions in large bowl.  Cover and chill.  Before serving, stir together salt, pepper and mayonnaise. Toss with rice mixture.  Spoon over lettuce, garnish with lemon and tomato wedges.    Crabmeat and lobster or combination of three may be used.   July 25, 1991

------------------------

## 948203 -- CARIBBEAN  SHRIMP  AND  BLACK  BEAN  SALAD

1 lb. cooked shrimp
1 (15 oz.) can black beans, rinsed &
    drained
1 green pepper, cut into strips
1/2 c. sliced celery
1 med. onion, cut into rings
2/3 c. picante sauce
2 tbsp. chopped cilantro
2 tbsp. vegetable oil
2 tbsp. honey
1 tsp. grated lime peel
2 tbsp. fresh lime juice
Garnish with 1 c. cherry tomato
     halves & lettuce leaves

Combine shrimp, beans, green pepper, celery and onion in large bowl.  Combine remaining ingredients and mix well.  Pour over shrimp, mix and toss lightly to coat.  Cover and chill at least 2 hours, lightly tossing once.  Spoon salad into lettuce lined serving platter in individual plates.  Garnish with tomatoes.  September 24, 1992

------------------------

## 948204 -- SHRIMP   SALAD

1 pkg. shell macaroni
1 pkg. frozen shrimp
1/2 c. mayonnaise
1/4 c. French dressing
1/4 tsp. garlic powder
Dash of pepper
Dash of paprika
1 tbsp. onion flakes

Cook shrimp according to directions, combine with other ingredients.   Chill at least 4 hours to receive the best flavor. You can add chopped celery and olives, if desired.

------------------------

### 948205 -- SALMON RICE SALAD

2 c. Carolina rice, cooked & cooled
1 c. celery, sliced
1/2 c. green onion, sliced
1/2 c. sweet pickle relish
1 c. salad dressing
1/2 tsp. black pepper
2 (6 1/8 oz.) cans Chicken of the Sea
    skinless boneless pink salmon
1/2 c. red pepper, chopped
1/2 c. pine nuts
1 c. frozen peas, thawed
Lettuce leaves

Combine all ingredients and toss gently. Chill. Serves 6.

------------------------

### 948206 -- SEAFOOD BISQUE

1/2 c. onion, chopped
1/2 c. celery, sliced
1/4 c. butter
1/2 c. flour
4 1/2 c. water
1 chicken bouillon cube
1 tbsp. ketchup
1 bay leaf
1 tsp. seasoned salt
1 1/2 c. (two 6 oz. cans) crab meat
    or shrimp and juice
1 c. undiluted evaporated milk

Saute onion and celery in butter in large saucepan. Stir in flour. Gradually stir in water. Add bouillon cube, ketchup, bay leaf and seasoning salt. Heat to boiling; reduce heat and boil gently 5 minutes. Add seafood and juice; stir to break up meat. Boil gently 5 minutes. Discard bay leaf. Stir in evaporated milk. Reheat to serving temperature; do not boil. Makes 7 1/2 cups.

------------------------

## 948207 -- SEAFOOD PASTA SALAD

1/2 c. Miracle Whip salad dressing
1/4 c. Kraft "Zesty" Italian dressing
2 tbsp. Kraft 100% grated Parmesan
   cheese
2 c. (8 oz.) corkscrew noodles,
   cooked, drained
1 1/2 c. (8 oz.) imitation crabmeat,
   chopped
1 c. broccoli flowerettes, partially
   cooked
1/2 c. tomato, chopped
1/4 c. green onion, sliced
1/2 c. green pepper, chopped
   (optional)

Combine dressings and cheese; mix well. Add remaining ingredients; mix lightly. Chill.

------------------------

## 948208 -- MACARONI SALAD WITH SHRIMP

4 c. cooked shell macaroni
3 c. chopped shrimp (pre-boiled in
   seasonings)
1 onion, finely chopped
1/2 c. finely chopped celery
1/4 c. green pepper, chopped
5 hard-boiled eggs, chopped
1 c. mayonnaise or salad dressing
   (may use half mayonnaise & half
   salad dressing)

Combine all ingredients, cover and chill overnight. Yield: 10 to 12 servings.

------------------------

## 948209 -- SHRIMP REMOULADE

2 hard-cooked eggs, mashed
2 sticks celery, minced
1 tsp. Worcestershire sauce
2 tbsp. sauterne (table)
3 tbsp. mustard

8 tbsp. Zatarain's creole mustard
1 pt. mayonnaise
1 tsp. salt
1/2 tsp. pepper
1 tbsp. sugar
3 tbsp. grated onion
Juice of lemon
2 cans shrimp or fresh boiled shrimp

Mix all ingredients together and serve over lettuce and tomatoes.

------------------------

## 948210 -- GRAPEFRUIT AND SHRIMP SALAD

4 1/2 c. water
1 1/2 lbs. unpeeled, sm. fresh
    shrimp, uncooked
4 pink grapefruits
Bibb lettuce
4 hard cooked eggs, chopped
1/2 c. mayonnaise
1/4 c. catsup
1 tbsp. plus 1 tsp. pickle relish
1/8 tsp. white pepper

Bring water to a boil, add shrimp. Cook 3 to 5 minutes. Drain well and rinse with cold water. Peel and devein shrimp. To make grapefruit shells, use 1 grapefruit for each bowl. Cut a thin slice from stem end of each grapefruit to level the base. Score rind with sharp knife to make a shell with 4 petals, starting about 2 inches from top of grapefruit and ending within 2 inches of base. Then cut just through the rind along scoring. Carefully pull each petal from fruit, using a grapefruit knife to separate pulp from rind. Remove grapefruit pulp intact using thumb to dislodge pulp; set shell half of grapefruit shells with lettuce; spoon grapefruit into shell. Combine eggs, mayonnaise, catsup, pickle relish and pepper; spoon over grapefruit. Top with shrimp. Yield 4 servings. This salad is one of my favorites. Serve it with a fish dinner and your guest will love it.

------------------------

## 948211 -- SHRIMP GAZPACHO

2 garlic cloves, chopped
2 tbsp. olive oil
2 tbsp. red wine vinegar
2 tbsp. fresh lemon juice

1/2 lb. cooked lg. shrimp, peeled & deveined
3/4 lb. lg. plum tomatoes (about 6), seeded, chopped
1 green bell pepper, chopped
1 red bell pepper, chopped
1/2 lg. cucumber, peeled, seeded, chopped
1 bunch green onions, chopped
1/2 bunch fresh cilantro leaves, chopped
1 lg. Jalapeno chili, minced
4 1/2 c. tomato juice, chilled
Lemon wedges

Combine first 4 ingredients in medium bowl. Add shrimp; cover mixture and refrigerate 1 to 2 hours. Combine tomatoes, green and red pepper, cucumber, green onions, cilantro and Jalapeno in large bowl. Add tomato juice. Stir in shrimp mixture. Season to taste with salt and pepper. Garnish with lemon wedges. 6 servings. My family adores seafood and likes Gazpacho, so I thought it was a good idea to make it different then the usual. Think your family and guests will find it wonderful also.

------------------------

948213 --

2 tbsp. butter
1 med. chopped onion
1 med. finely chopped pepper
2 c. corn kernels, frozen
2 c. chicken broth
1 c. half & half
1 c. corn kernels
3/4 lb. med. shrimp, peeled, deveined & cut into 3/4 inch pieces
1 tsp. salt
1/2 c. fresh cilantro leaves, chopped

In a large, heavy skillet, melt butter. When it has foamed, stir in onion and let soften 3 to 4 minutes. Add green pepper and continue cooking another 3 to 4 minutes. Puree 2 cups corn in food processor, scrape into skillet. Stir in stock and half and half and let simmer 2 to 3 minutes. Stir in remaining corn, shrimp, salt, pepper until shrimp are just cooked through. Taste for seasonings, then ladle the soup into bowls and garnish with extra cilantro leaves.

------------------------

## 948214 -- EASY SHRIMP SALAD

4 qt. saucepan
1 lg. mixing bowl
1 lb. ditalini-Ronzoni product
Hellmann's mayonnaise
1 lg. green bell pepper, diced
4 cans of shrimp
Salt
Black pepper

Cook ditalini as directed, drain and cool. Combine in the large mixing bowl the following: mayonnaise, salt and pepper, ditalini and green pepper. When this is combined well, add the shrimp, but do gently so not to break the tiny shrimp. Cover and put into refrigerator. Serve as a side dish or a bar-b-que.

------------------------

## 948215 -- POTATO - SALMON CHOWDER

4 c. peeled potatoes, cut in 1/2 inch
   cubes
1 c. sliced carrots
1 tbsp. salt
3 c. water
1 (10 oz.) pkg. frozen peas
1/2 tsp. Worcestershire sauce
1/2 c. margarine
1/3 c. chopped onion
1/4 c. flour
5 c. milk
1 lb. can salmon
1 c. celery, thinly sliced

Cook potatoes and carrots in salted water until just tender. Add frozen peas. Bring to boil, cook 1 minute. Remove from heat, do not drain. Melt margarine in skillet. Add onion, cook until lightly browned. Add flour, stir until smooth. Cook 1 minute. Add 1/2 the milk, stirring constantly. Cook over low heat until sauce boils and thickens. Flake salmon, add to vegetables. Add hot white sauce, celery, Worcestershire sauce and remaining milk to vegetables and salmon. Heat thoroughly. Serve at once. Makes 3 quarts.

------------------------

## 948216 -- BALTIMORE CRAB STEW

1 lb. crab meat
1 tsp. salt
1 tsp. white pepper
1 tbsp. butter
1 pt. milk
1 pt. light cream
1/2 tsp. Tabasco sauce or more to taste
1 tsp. Worcestershire sauce
6 tbsp. sherry

Bring crab, salt, pepper, butter and milk to a slow simmer; let simmer very slowly for 10 minutes. Add cream and sauces. Bring to boiling point, but do not boil. Stir as little as possible so as not to break up crab meat. Add sherry; let stand just a moment. Remove from burner. Serve in warm cups topped with lemon slices and chopped parsley. Serves about 4. A great Superbowl soup!

------------------------

948217 -- HOT CRAB SALAD

1 lb. flaked crab meat (2 c.)
1 c. sliced celery
1/2 c. minced green pepper
2 hard-cooked eggs, chopped
1 c. mayonnaise
1 tbsp. lemon juice
1 tbsp. Worcestershire sauce
3/4 c. fine soft bread crumbs
2 tbsp. melted butter

Combine crab, celery, green pepper, eggs, mayonnaise, lemon juice and Worcestershire. Turn into buttered 1 1/2 quart baking dish. Top with crumbs mixed with butter. Bake at 325 degrees for 30 minutes. Serves 4.

------------------------

948218 -- SEAFOOD SALAD

1 lb. cleaned shrimp
1 lb. cleaned squid
1 lb. sea scallops
Italian parsley, chopped
Fresh thyme
4 cloves fresh garlic, chopped

3 oz. virgin olive oil
The juice from 2 fresh lemons
Salt
Pepper

Poach all seafood. Slice into small morsels. Mix in remaining ingredients. Serve cold. Serves 12.

------------------------

### 948219 -- SEAFOOD DELIGHT

1 lb. shrimp, scallops, crab, lobster, conch
Bacon (streaks of lean, streaks of fat)
1 lg. bell pepper
Onion
Thyme or bay leaf
Old Bay seasoning
Red cooking wine
1 can cream style corn
Rice or pasta

Cut in chunks. Stir-fry conch, scallops, lobster and crab along with the bacon until the bacon is brown. Then add onions, then bell pepper. When all these ingredients are done to taste, add shrimp for the last 2 to 3 minutes of cooking. After which, add 1 cup of red wine and stir-fry for about 2 minutes. Remove to a large pot and add can of corn. Let cook for about 15 minutes. Serve over rice or pasta. Serve with garlic bread to top this fantastic meal.

------------------------

### 948220 -- SEAFOOD SOUP

3 cans beef broth
6 c. water
1/4 c. onion, chopped
2 tsp. Old Bay
1 can tomatoes
2 pkgs. frozen mixed vegetables
5 c. potatoes, sliced
1 lb. crab meat
1 lb. shrimp
1 lb. conch

In large soup pot, combine beef broth, water, onion and Old Bay seasoning; bring to a boil. Add tomatoes, mixed vegetables and potatoes; simmer 1 1/2 hours. Stir in seafood; simmer 1 1/2 hours. Makes 10 to 12 servings.

------------------------

948221 -- MY VERY OWN SHRIMP SALAD

1 lb. pkg. petite shrimp
1 c. celery, diced
1/8 tsp. pepper
Lettuce
3 hard cooked eggs, diced
1/3 c. mayonnaise or salad dressing
1/2 tsp. salt
1 green pepper, chopped

Rinse shrimp. Combine all the ingredients and serve on lettuce. Crab meat may be used instead of shrimp.

------------------------

948226 -- BUTTERNUT SQUASH & SHRIMP BISQUE

1/2 stick butter
1 c. diced onion
1/4 c. plain flour
3 c. chicken stock
3 c. peeled & diced butternut squash
3 bay leaves
1 can cream of chicken or celery soup
1 c. whipping cream
1 lb. sm. peeled, uncooked shrimp

Melt butter in heavy large saucepan, over medium-low heat. Add onion and cook until transparent, stir occasionally for about 10 minutes. Add flour and stir 3 minutes. Add stock and bring to a boil, stir constantly. Add squash and bay leaves, simmer until squash is very tender about 15 minutes. Blend in can of soup and whipping cream. Season to taste and remove bay leaves. Puree soup in blender. Before serving, add shrimp and heat on low. Pumpkin can be substituted for squash. Sprinkle with nutmeg.

------------------------

www.ingramcontent.com/pod-product-compliance
Lightning Source LLC
Chambersburg PA
CBHW081419080526
44589CB00016B/2595